DINNER IN THE DINER

A history of railway catering

Neil Wooler
with a foreword by
Prue Leith

David & Charles
Newton Abbot   London   North Pomfret (Vt)

For the men and women, of all ages,
by whose efforts Britain's railway
passengers travel refreshed

British Library Cataloguing in Publication Data
Wooler, Neil
  Dinner in the diner.
  1. Railways – Great Britain – Dining-car
  service – History
  I. title
  385′.2   TF668

  ISBN 0–7153–8796–0

Photoset by Northern Phototypesetting Co, Bolton
and printed in Great Britain
by Redwood Burn Limited, Trowbridge
for David & Charles Publishers plc
Brunel House Newton Abbot Devon

Published in the United States of America
By David & Charles Inc
North Pomfret Vermont 05053 USA

Contents

Foreword

by Prue Leith

Not long ago the BBC television programme, *Food and Drink*, asked me if I'd like to think up some buffet dishes to be sold on the trains. Wonderful. At last the chance to do what every member of the British public wants to do – to show British Rail how to do its job.

Well, I had the satisfaction of seeing my Spicy Bean and Sausage Hot-Pot and my Pasta shells with tomato and cheese sell moderately well; but I also learnt what I had failed to learn during the eight years I had sat as a non-executive director on the former Travellers-Fare Board, and in five years on the British Rail main Board – namely, that being a BR steward is hard work. First of all, you get seasick standing up. Secondly, the loaded trolleys are very heavy and have a will of their own, arbitrarily snagging the passengers' luggage and running over your toes. And thirdly, after four hours or so your legs ache, your back aches and your feet feel like balloons.

The fact is, it is hard to stay confidently critical of any organisation unless you keep your distance, carefully preserving your ignorance. Only people who have not bought a British Rail sandwich in 15 years talk of curly ones. Only someone who knows nothing whatever about rail catering thinks there is a fortune to be made out of it.

But there is the other danger, that of getting too close. I remember when I had recently joined Travellers-Fare and was at a gathering of British Rail passengers I was asked the already familiar question, 'Why does the coffee have to be so awful on trains?' I went confidently into my routine about the British public drinking 'instant' in preference to real coffee at home; about the prohibitive cost of china cups; about jolly hooligans throwing them onto the track; and so on. My questioner interrupted: 'How long have you been with Travellers-Fare?'

'Six months', I answered. 'Well you should quit', he said; 'you have been nobbled.' He was right: knowing the *reasons* why the coffee is not good does not make it any better.

Yet Neil Wooler, who was as close as anyone can be to railway catering without actually frying the bacon, has managed a book that has enough distance to be objective, and enough proximity to be highly informative. It is a laudable achievement. He has managed to give us a readable pacy history of train and station catering, from the times when Brunel complained about the coffee on Swindon station to today, with fascinating excursions into the portals of the grand railway hotels, into the wine cellars under Derby headquarters, and through the famous Royal Trains. Before *Dinner in the Diner* there was a gap in the literature of the railways; Neil Wooler has filled it admirably.

Introduction

What is the magic that dinner in the diner, at its best, can distil so potently?

Upon the platform of some great railway junction like York or Carlisle, waiting travellers stand and gaze as a non-stop express sweeps by, the figures within the lighted windows joining some seemingly enchanted feast as their dining car bears them northward into the night. On board, the mystique is equally compelling as with stewards bustling deftly around the fortunate passengers tuck into their repast while the restaurant car, crockery enticingly a-jingle, speeds its way past hill and dale.

All this may sound a shade pretentious; yet there are many who readily confess to feeling just this way about dining on a train. Of course, a summer journey along that magnificent line atop the Northumbrian cliffs or through the mountain fastness of the Scottish Highlands can but heighten the diner's sense of delicious civilisation, but even the industrial Midlands on a dank February day seem to assume a rosier aspect in the warm afterglow of breakfast in a well-stocked restaurant car. No other form of transport, however glamorous, offers quite the same blend of fascination and romance.

Yet at the same time, in a way unique to our society, this remarkable business has acquired a 'downside' as deeply ingrained in British folklore as mothers-in-law. Surely no other institution in our life has produced, over a century and more, such a love–hate relationship. Is this because of some grave disappointment on a journey otherwise long since forgotten, such as when the promised service of dinner simply did not materialise? Is it because the buffet car, rendezvous for the majority of today's travellers, offers a rather less beguiling ambience of long queues and instant coffee? Or is it all the fault of the newspapers? Certainly the 'Aunt Sally' attitude, impervious to rationality, still pervades many a journalist's column. Perhaps it is a mixture of all these. But for all the attention focussed for good or ill upon it, the dining car is only a part of the much wider story of railway hospitality.

The railway hotels, recalled with affection by many a fashionable traveller, were a rather different world, albeit one under the same management. Sadly the past tense is appropriate here, for although many of them are still very much in business, railway hotels as a group are now part of history. But the mark made upon British life by their imposing presence, both above and below stairs, is a substantial story in itself. In a book dedicated first and foremost to railway catering, I have had to take care not to let the tail wag the dog. Although the hotels started life very much as an integral part of rail travel, they began as the decades passed to go more and more their separate ways. Latterly indeed, new visitors to places out of sight of the contemporary railway network, like Turnberry maybe, Moretonhampstead, or even world-famous Gleneagles, often never realised that these were indeed railway establishments.

Some of these fine places have now been re-sold, not once, but three or four times, since the break-up of British Transport Hotels in 1983. That change in some of them was overdue cannot be denied, but the abrupt end (in some cases) to proud traditions, for reasons far removed from the concept of service which was their hallmark, is a sad if typical reflection of the tone of the times we live in.

And then there are the station refreshment rooms, for generations the butt of music-hall comics with their well-worn sandwich jokes, yet ever more profitable than either hotels or dining cars. Recent years have witnessed a transformation of the station buffet scene, but for a long time these places seemed to hark back to those bad old days when Charles Dickens railed against them in his novels. Why? What was it, exactly, that Dickens wrote? How did the prejudice surrounding 'railway refreshments' become so deeply ingrained in our national psyche? And just what in fact did the railway traveller eat in those days? The answers to these questions, and more, I hope, lie in the following pages.

Today the pace of change in the business is such that even as this book was working its way through to publication, new developments began to overtake several of the practices I have written about in the present tense. One cannot always foretell, though, whether today's bright ideas will end up in tomorrow's waste paper baskets or prove to have more lasting significance. Moreover, the politics and personalities of the immediate past represent a veritable minefield for any writer, as well as lacking the truer perspective that time affords. For these reasons I have felt it wise to confine the story of recent years to a strictly factual and straightforward account of principal events.

Among the myriad volumes and histories that fill today's railway bookshelves, the catering and hotels story figures hardly at all. This is a surprising state of affairs for such a public topic, and one brought forcibly home to me when, as PR man for the business, I was faced during the 1979 restaurant car centenary and after with a welter of enquiries from writers all over the world about this fascinating saga. The story is one of social, transport, culinary, political, and not least human interest, and this book is an attempt to fill at least a little of that gap. A great deal of enjoyable research has gone into it, and I hope that any omissions or inaccuracies are not so serious as to spoil the end result.

These pages may perhaps jog some memories of vanished times, be they golden glimpses of childhood journeys, or the very different flashbacks to the struggles and shortages of drab post-war austerity. Even there time seems to have filtered out hard reality, leaving a fashionable nostalgia that today regularly appears in theatre and on television. Possibly that is for the best, but if this book records the good and bad of one strand of public life through those times, and maybe stirs in the older reader's mind some half-forgotten railborne memory that was in danger of being lost for good, then it will not have been in vain.

L. N. S. Wooler
Weston Favell, Northampton
December 1986.

1
Early Days

The notice in the timetable allowed for no misunderstanding:

"No person will be allowed to sell eatables of any kind upon the Line. The Company earnestly hope that the public will co-operate with them in enforcing this regulation as it will be the means of removing a cause of delay."

The year was 1837 – the year in which Queen Victoria began her long reign over Britain's industrial high summer. That company was the Grand Junction Railway, the country's first trunk line, newly opened from Birmingham to Manchester and Liverpool. The notice clearly signalled that a new problem was facing those who operated public transport – and those who travelled by it, too – the problem of feeding and watering large numbers of people, while at the same time carrying them to their destinations with all possible speed.

Just seven years earlier, passenger railways had been born with the opening of the Liverpool & Manchester Railway, the first line in the world to be planned and built with the carrying of people as well as goods in mind from the start. As the world knows, the Liverpool & Manchester was an immediate success. Yet almost from the first day a conflict of interests had begun to show itself; on the one hand there were the staff trying to operate a railway timetable, and on the other local vendors and innkeepers eager to ply their wares to this new and hungry market running past their doorsteps. The passengers no doubt, as passengers will, hoped for the best of both worlds. A Liverpool & Manchester Board meeting of 1837 fulminated about the "inconvenience and nuisance of the existing practice of hawking about Eccles cakes and Ale and Spirit to railway passengers at almost every stopping place between Warrington Junction and Manchester." They decided to ban it, and this edict must have worked, for records show the proprietors of the Chat Moss

Tavern, in November that year, re-applying for permission to serve passengers on the trains. They didn't get it.

Before the coming of the railways, the highest form of passenger travel had been the stagecoach with its maximum load of a score or so, and its need to stop regularly to change horses. It was under these conditions that the tradition of the great coaching inns grew up, where passengers would partake of refreshment while horses were changed. The largest inns might sometimes have several coaches in at once, but the number of customers they brought was still small enough for them to be served in time-honoured ways. For this was before the days of the inn bar, and customers would sit at tables with their tankards and plates while the landlord would bring round foaming jugs of 'home-brewed', from his brewhouse out the back.

It was just such a place that was to be the very first house of railway refreshment. It was built not by a passenger line, but by the coal-carrying Garnkirk & Glasgow Railway in Central

The platform hawker plies his wares of meat pies and pop. An illustration by the Victorian humourist Cuthbert Bede from *Little Mr Bouncer and his friend, Verdant Green* (1873).

Scotland – an early railway that has remained surprisingly little known south of the border. The Garnkirk & Glasgow had opened in 1831 to carry coal from the collieries around the district of Airdrie to the city of Glasgow, ten miles distant. It was the first public railway to run into that city, and it quickly began to attract numbers of Glaswegians eager to make their very first railway journey, riding in a coal wagon if necessary. However, on arrival at Gartsherrie, at the 'country' end of the line, these trippers would often be faced with a substantial wait for a train back, and little in the way of entertainment to hand save viewing the local coal tips. So with good Scottish initiative, and not a little hope, the Garnkirk & Glasgow decided to try and cash in on the situation by making something of Gartsherrie as an attractive destination in its own right. The Gartsherrie Inn was accordingly built, and on 10 July 1832 this advertisement appeared in the *Glasgow Courier*:

'The Railway Company, having understood that inconvenience was experienced by Passengers visiting the Railway, for the want of accommodation at its eastern extremity, have erected a commodious Inn at Gargill, which is newly opened by Mr Wilson, late of the Caledonian Inn, Glasgow, under whose active and judicious management every convenience is afforded.'

The Gartsherrie Inn was to undergo a change of management in just three years, for on 18 July 1835 an advertisement in the *Glasgow Herald* announced that 'George Clark, late of the Anchor Tavern, Trongate . . . has removed to Gartsherrie Inn, which is entirely new furnished. He has laid in a choice selection of Wines, Spirits, Ales, &c, and hopes by assiduity and attention to merit a continuance of public favour.'

The Gartsherrie remained in business as an inn only until 1843, when the Garnkirk & Glasgow Railway accounts show an expenditure of £6 18s 3d (£6·91) for its 'alteration to dwelling-houses'. However, from a photograph taken in 1930 it seems that comestibles of some kind were still on sale there even then.

As the 1830s unfolded, so began the completion of much longer-distance lines than the Garnkirk & Glasgow, and it soon became more than clear that stagecoach traditions were no longer enough. Along the 30-odd-mile length of the Liverpool & Manchester Railway, opened in 1830, dozens of budding local catering entrepreneurs welcomed the new market that the

Where it all began: the Gartsherrie Inn, Garnkirk & Glasgow Railway, photographed in 1931 long after conversion to a dwelling-house, though still apparently selling basic provisions. The building was demolished in the 1960s. *J. F. McEwan.*

passenger trains offered every time they stopped. A *Manchester City News* article of the day describes the scene:

> 'At Eccles, trays were "poked" at the Passengers filled with the cakes then famous' [one assumes the writer meant that the trays were filled, rather than the passengers] 'and at Newton, where an hotel of note was situated near the line, the same attention was paid; "home-brewed" and sandwiches were carried by waiters along the length of the train, in imitation of the stage-coach custom.'

As we have seen, this kind of thing was threatening to play havoc with the railway timetable and arouse the ire of the Board. So it was no surprise that when the Grand Junction Railway opened, with a main line northward from Birmingham three times the length of the Liverpool & Manchester, the GJR Board should have been most concerned to do everything to keep down these delays. Accordingly it published the stern notice that begins this book, but it failed at least for a time to do the more constructive thing and actually open its own eating house, where passengers could be fed in better-organised and less time-consuming fashion. This need must have been in the mind of the writer of *Osborne's Guide to the Grand Junction Railway*, published in 1838, the year following the line's opening. At this stage, the railway was still operating out of a temporary terminus in Birmingham, and Osborne, in that indigestible prose beloved of our forefathers, commented:

> 'There is another thing, which though not at present publicly projected, nor even hinted at, that we know of, is yet generally felt to be needed: a Railroad Tavern; where the principles which regulate the payments of the road, will be applied to the payments of the Inn. . . . A small approach to this system is already made, by a provision of Breakfast for the passengers by the early train, at the Temporary Station.'

No mention of catering facilities as such appears anywhere in Osborne's *'Guide'*, so the 'provision of Breakfast' probably came from some neighbouring Birmingham hostelry – very likely Dee's Royal Hotel in nearby Temple Row, a place prominently advertised in the Guide as being 'patronised by Her Majesty; HRH the Duchess of Kent; HRH the Duke of Sussex, etc, etc.'

It was certainly Mr Dee himself who in the following year became the proprietor of the very first railway refreshment room. In May 1838 the London & Birmingham Railway opened its station a short distance away at Curzon Street. This railway, with its 113-mile main line, was the first to recognise the need to provide proper catering for its passengers from the word go, and built refreshment rooms at both ends of the line (though the London one, incorporated in an hotel, did not open till the following year) and at roughly the halfway point of Wolverton.

The one at Birmingham Curzon Street may well have opened with the station in May 1838. At the time of this opening, London-bound trains only travelled as far as Rugby, because work had still not finished on the great Kilsby Tunnel beyond; passengers had to travel thence by horse-drawn coach to Denbigh Hall, near Bletchley, there to entrain once more for London. Through running between Birmingham and London finally began on 17 September 1838, and the following day *The Times*, commenting upon this opening, reported:

'The lower portion of the magnificent station house in Birmingham has recently been licensed as an hotel to Mr Dee, Mine host of The Royal, so that passengers, if they think proper, may be accommodated with every good thing without leaving the company's premises. The innkeepers of the town complain of this establishment, in company with the station-house, as a monopoly; but we presume that the immense influx of passengers into Birmingham, as evidenced this day, which will be occasioned by the entire opening of the railway, will speedily render these complaints uncalled-for.'

The refreshment rooms at the halfway point of Wolverton, though not mentioned in *The Times* article, were opened by March 1839 and trains stopped there for some minutes, allowing cold and hungry passengers to revive themselves. These Wolverton rooms have achieved a place in history through the description written by Francis Bond Head, a freelance journalist who published a highly entertaining account of what had by then become the London & North Western Railway, under the title *Stokers and Pokers*.

Head's description was written in 1849, when the refreshment rooms had been open ten years. At first a local caterer provided the service there, but by November 1839 complaints were being received about the quality of the food, and this caterer was quietly moved out. These complaints may have stemmed from the hurried way in which passengers had to cram down their victuals. The trouble may have been, as we have observed before, that no-one had yet mastered the technique of serving large numbers of people at once; and it may have been that the resources at Wolverton, a new industrial town still in the process of being planted upon rural Buckinghamshire by the railway company, were not yet sufficient for the job. At all events, the Wolverton catering contract was re-let in January 1840 to Messrs Dethier & Vantini, a firm which had taken on the running of the company's hotels at Euston in London. By the time of *Stokers and Pokers*, Dethier's manageress in charge at Wolverton was one Mrs Leonora Hibbert, a redoubtable lady soon to earn promotion to the port of Holyhead where the London & North Western Railway was busy developing facilities for the Irish boat traffic.

Head's account of Wolverton has been quoted many times since then, but its whimsical yet detailed description remains unsurpassed as a document of a special piece of Victorian life. We should remember that because Wolverton town was built from scratch in rural surroundings labour had to be recruited from many different areas, and living accommodation had to be built or provided for those who worked there – the more so in the case of the refreshment rooms, because of the youthful and vulnerable nature of the female staff (and no doubt the proximity of lusty apprentices at the railway workshops down the road).

'The refreshment establishment at Wolverton', wrote Head, 'is composed of:
1. A matron or *generallissima*.
2. Seven very young ladies to wait upon the passengers.
3. Four men and three boys   do   do.
4. One man-cook, his kitchen-maid, and his two scullery-maids.
5. Two housemaids.
6. One still-room maid, employed solely in the liquid duty of making tea and coffee.
7. Two laundry-maids.
8. One baker and one baker's boy.
9. One garden-boy.
And lastly, what is most significantly described in the books of establishment—
10. An "odd-man".'
There are also 85 pigs and piglings, of whom hereafter.
  'Very early in the morning – in cold winter, long before sunrise – the "odd-man" wakens the two house maids, to one of whom is intrusted the confidential duty of wakening the seven young ladies at exactly seven o'clock, in order that their "premiere toilette" may be concluded in time for them to receive the passengers of the first train, which reaches Wolverton at 7.30 a.m. From that time until the departure of . . . The York Mail train . . . at about eleven o'clock at night, these young persons remain on duty; continually vibrating, at the ringing of a bell, across the rails (they have a covered passage high above them, but they never use it) from the North refreshment room for Down passengers to the South refreshment room constructed for hungry Up ones. By about Midnight . . . they are all enabled once again to lay their heads upon their pillows, with the exception of one, who assisted by one man and one boy . . . remains on duty receiving the money, &c., till four in the morning for the Up-Mail. The young person, however, who in her weekly turn performs this extra task, instead of rising with the others at seven, is allowed to sleep on till noon.
  'The scene on the arrival of every train . . . need hardly be described. As these youthful handmaidens stand in a row behind bright silver urns, silver coffee pots, silver tea pots, cups, saucers,

cakes, sugar, milk, with other delicacies over which they preside, the confused crowd of passengers simultaneously liberated from the train hurry towards them with a velocity exactly proportionate to their appetites. The hungriest face enters the door first, followed by a crowd very much resembling, in eagerness and joyous independence, the rush at the prorogation of Parliament . . . to the bar of what they mysteriously call "another place".

'Considering that the row of young persons have among them all only seven right hands, with but very little fingers at the end of each, it is really astonishing how . . . they can in the space of a few minutes manage to extend and withdraw them so often – sometimes to give a cup of tea – sometimes to receive half a crown, of which they have to return two shillings – then to give an old gentleman a plate of warm soup – then to drop another lump of sugar into his nephew's coffee cup – then to receive a penny for a bun, and then again threepence for four "lady's fingers".

'It is their rule as well as their desire never, if they can possibly prevent it, to speak to anyone; and although sometimes, when thunder has turned the milk, or the kitchen-maid over-peppered the soup, it may occasionally be necessary to soothe the fastidious complaints of some beardless ensign by an infinitesimal appeal to the generous feelings of his nature – we mean, by the hundred-thousandth part of a smile – yet they endeavour on no account ever to exceed that harmless dose.

'But while they are thus occupied at the centre of the refreshment table, at its two ends, each close to a warm stove, a very plain matter-of-fact business is going on, which consists of the rapid uncorking of, and then emptying into large tumblers, innumerable black bottles of what is not unappropriately called "Stout", inasmuch as all the persons who are drinking the dark foam mixture wear heavy great-coats, with large wrappers round their necks – in fact, are *very* stout.

'But the bell is violently calling the passengers to "Come! Come away!" and as they have all paid their fares, and as the engine is loudly hissing . . . they soon, like the swallows of summer, congregate together and fly away.

'It appears from the books that the annual consumption at the refreshment-room averages—

182,500 Banbury cakes	5,110 lb moist sugar	
56,940 Queen cakes	16,425 quarts of milk	
29,200 patés	1,095 ,, ,, cream	
36,500 lb of flour	8,088 bottles of lemonade	
13,140 ,, ,, butter	10,416 ,, ,, soda water	
2,920 ,, ,, coffee	45,012 ,, ,, stout	
43,800 ,, ,, meat	25,692 ,, ,, ale	
5,110 ,, ,, currants	5,208 ,, ,, ginger beer	
1,277 ,, ,, tea	547 ,, ,, port	
5,840 ,, ,, loaf sugar	2,095 ,, ,, sherry	

And we regret to add,
    666 bottles of gin
    464   ,,   ,, rum
2,392   ,,   ,, brandy.
'To the eatables are to be added, or driven, the 85 pigs, who after
having been from their birth most kindly treated and most
luxuriously fed, are impartially promoted, by seniority, one after
another into an infinite number of pork pies.'

Doubtless these porcine denizens of Wolverton enjoyed a rich
and copious diet of swill from the very refreshment rooms where
they were employed. In today's conservation-conscious times,
this early example of thrifty re-cycling is surely something that
commends itself anew.

Head rounds off his masterly accounts with a necessary word
as to the character of those seven very young ladies:

'Considering the temptations to which they are constantly exposed,
in offering to the public attentions which are ever to simmer and yet
never to boil – it might be expected that our enquiries should
considerately go no further than the arrival at 11 p.m. of the up York
Mail. The excellent matron, however, who has charge of these young
people – who always dine and live at her table – with honest pride
declares, that the breath of slander has never ventured to sully the
reputation of any of those who have been committed to her charge;
and as this testimony is corroborated by persons residing in the
neighbourhood and very capable of observation, we cannot take
leave of the establishment without expressing our appreciation of
the good sense and attention with which it is conducted.'

But Matron Leonora Hibbert must occasionally have been
looking the other way, for Head adds a postscript: 'We quite
forgot to mention that, notwithstanding the everlasting hurry
at this establishment, four of the young attendants have
managed to make excellent marriages and are now very well off
in the world.'

Such was life behind the scenes at one of Britain's earliest
railway refreshment rooms. For the youngsters, probably
hardly into their teens, things must have been a little akin to the
old-fashioned boarding school – the dormitories, the discipline,
and not least that ever-ringing bell, whose sound must have
become indelibly printed in the minds of all who spent their first
days away from home at establishments such as Wolverton.

The travelling public, however, was in general rather more

The hustle and hassle of the old-time refreshment scene, captured by cartoonist Leech in *Punch*'s annual Almanack for 1856.

interested in things as seen from its side of the counter. In particular, the heat of the soup effectively prevented it being consumed in the time allowed. In 1845 this complaint entered history in an issue of *Punch*: 'We defy any Soup to be so red-hot, so scorchingly and intensely sacrifying to the roof of the mouth, as the Soup you are allowed just three minutes to swallow at the Wolverton Station of the London and Birmingham Railway.'

Scarifyingly hot the soup may have been, but at least there was no suggestion here of the sharp practice employed in similar circumstances at Tonbridge, and recounted here by the contemporary Victorian writer F. S. Williams:

'A train on the South Eastern line stopped at Tonbridge station, and the passengers rushed out to obtain some refreshment. They had hardly begun to sip their hot coffee, when the bell rang, and the exclamation of the Guard, "Now, gentlemen, take your places, if you please," compelled them, however reluctantly, to resume their seats. But from some cause or other, the train did not start for several minutes, and before it left the station the travellers had the pleasure of seeing their almost brimming cups which they had left on the counter, emptied back into the urns for the next customers. As they rolled away, one of them made an estimate of how many times the same cup might thus be calculated to serve before it was finally consumed; but the result of this calculation, like many other theories, had better pass away without a record.'

This little piece of skulduggery seems to have caught the imagination of the public of the day, and very possibly of the caterers as well, for similar tales of everlasting coffee, or tea, or soup, are recorded about various other places in the popular literature of the times. Certainly there have always been temptations to cut corners, such as prolonging the life of a brew of tea, by dint of frequent top-ups of hot water, well beyond the point where the quality becomes unacceptable. This problem, incidentally, has on the trains themselves only been solved with the advent of instant tea, practical but of mixed popularity; this brew has a measured amount of tea solids in each cup, to which the attendant adds boiling water.

Poor tea may sometimes find its way to the customer when circumstances are difficult, as they certainly were in those early refreshment rooms. Bad coffee, however, is only too easy to make at any time. The stuff reacts at once to inexpert handling, even with today's sophisticated coffee-making machinery. Imagine what it was like in the days of primitive and unreliable urns and percolators. In 1841 the Great Western Railway, newly opened from London to Bristol, opened its famed refreshment rooms at Swindon and installed a truly magnificent silver percolator made in the form of a scale model of *Fire Fly*, one of Daniel Gooch's early broad-gauge locomotives. Impressive this piece of equipment was (and still is, for it survives in the Great Western Railway Museum at Swindon) but unfortunately the coffee it produced seems to have been of a rather different calibre. Brunel himself, the GWR's world-famed engineer, became very fed up with the situation and the lack of effectiveness of complaints, and in December 1842 he wrote to the contract caterer there as follows:

'Dear Sir, – I assure you Mr Player was wrong in supposing that I thought you purchased inferior coffee. I thought I said to him that I was surprised you should buy such bad roasted corn. I did not believe you had such a thing as coffee in the place; I am certain that I never tasted any. I have long ceased to make complaints at Swindon – I avoid taking anything there when I can help it.'

Thus Brunel – who, with a French-born father, must have grown up to expect good coffee – guaranteed the immortality of the Swindon refreshment rooms, beginning the joke about railway coffee that survives to this day. But the GWR

Garbage in, garbage out: poor beans tarnished the reputation of Swindon station's magnificent coffee urn, modelled on the locomotive *Fire Fly* by Messrs Martins of Cheltenham about 1840. *GWR Museum, Swindon.*

management did nothing to alleviate matters – rather the reverse, for it signed an agreement with the contractors there which virtually forced all the passengers to partake of the unsavoury brew themselves.

This agreement, which was to prove a millstone around the GWR's neck for fully 54 years, came about through the company's eagerness to seize what looked like a good bargain, coupled with a certain lack of foresight on the part of the directors. In 1841 the enterprising firm of builders, Messrs Joseph D. Rigby and Charles Rigby of Westminster, were engaged in building the railway line to Bristol, as well as several stations en route and a quantity of houses for railway workers in Swindon itself. This firm then undertook to erect, *at its own expense*, 'suitable refreshment rooms' at Swindon station, *provided that* 'all trains carrying passengers, not being goods trains, or trains to be sent express, or for special purposes', should stop at Swindon for the refreshment of passengers 'for a reasonable period of about ten minutes'. This agreement was to be valid for a term of 99 years from Christmas 1841. In addition to providing the rooms, the builders were to pay a peppercorn rent of one penny a year. For its part, the GWR undertook not only to stop all trains there, but to refrain from setting up any rival establishment along the line that might abstract from business at Swindon.

The premises, which straddled the main line with a connecting footbridge between, opened in July 1842, consisting not only of first and second class refreshment rooms but also an hotel (whose residents must have found the noise horrific). The lease further provided for a separate building across the courtyard 'for the use of workingmen and third class passengers'; this building survives as a pub to this day, as does the main structure of that on the westbound platform.

Rigby's, the builders, were clearly pleased with the bargain they had struck, and it soon proved that they had every right to be. The Great Western prospered as few beside Brunel himself had foreseen, and passengers at the compulsory Swindon stop swarmed into the refreshment room where the catering had quickly been sub-contracted to one S. Y. Griffiths of the Queen's Hotel, Cheltenham. This was (and is) a most upmarket establishment, but as we have seen, the coffee was not in quite the same league! Interestingly, the Hotel part of the Swindon building was to become known as the 'Queen's Royal Hotel,' very possibly after the Cheltenham connection, though in August 1848 the lease of it was sold on to a J. R. Phillips for the sum of £20,000.

Meanwhile, with the rapidly-developing quest for speed, the Great Western Railway was trying anxiously to divest itself of the incubus of that compulsory Swindon stop. In 1846 the company went to law to try to get the agreement nullified in the case of express trains. But Vice-Chancellor Wigram decided that the word 'express' as used in the contract did not mean what it usually means, but rather trains sent under some special agreement. In other words, the restrictions had been tightened still further!

This ruling was subsequently confirmed again by Lord Justice Mellish in another attempt by the GWR authorities 30 years later. In the meantime, the contract had changed hands several times, and in the words of the *Great Western Magazine*, 'proved so profitable that the original cost of the buildings having long since been defrayed and the rent being only one penny a year – that a limited liability company was formed, and the business was carried on in a much more ambitious style than was the case at the outset'.

'The Company', continues the magazine, 'still felt considerably the way in which their train service was handicapped by this "ten minutes at Swindon", and once more the Law Courts were appealed to. On this occasion it was agreed, by way of compromise, that mail trains should be regarded as being trains run for "special purposes", inasmuch as they carried mails by arrangement with the Postmaster-General, and that in the case of these trains, but these only, the period of detention at Swindon "for refreshments", should be reduced to five minutes, the other trains being detained the full period of ten minutes.'

This continued compromise still represented a major inconvenience to railway and passengers alike, and in August

The famous first class refreshment room at Swindon as it was in 1901. *GWR Museum, Swindon.*

1895 the Great Western Railway finally took the plunge and bought-out the lease for the enormous sum (in those days) of £100,000. In the 54 years since its signing, a succession of catering contractors had done very nicely, the railway had been forced to lag behind its rivals in terms of end-to-end journey speed, and countless thousands of passengers on 'God's Wonderful Railway' had been initiated into the secrets of the dreaded railway coffee.

All this did not stop a very considerable public relations job being done on behalf of the Swindon rooms. George Measom's classic *Illustrated Guide to The Great Western Railway*, published 1852 (and recently re-published in facsimile), describes the scene thus:

'Pleading a weakness towards banbury-cakes and sherry-cobler, we shall bend our steps towards the refreshment rooms, whose folding doors, and snug interior, tempt the passenger to while the few fleeting minutes allowed him, in procuring the services of the pretty and obliging Hebes that preside at the elegant and well provided counters under the superintendence of that paragon of caterers, Mr Phillips'.

More pretty and unblemished maidens – shades of Wolverton again here! But fair Hebe, in classical mythology the daughter of Jupiter and Juno (who is said to have conceived her after eating lettuces!) and the cup-bearer to all the gods, is said to have been dismissed from office by her father for falling down in an indecent posture at a grand feast. So possibly the young ladies of the Great Western did not quite match the unsullied brightness of their counterparts to the north. Measom continues:

'Every article of food, from a banbury-cake or a sandwich, to a basin of turtle or a cold fowl, – every assuager of thirst, from humble tea or bottled stout, to iced-lemonades or aristocratic champagne, is provided with a kind of heigh-presto rapidity, that might almost vie with the high railway speed, for which this great line has long and justly been celebrated.' The kitchens, he assures us, are 'filled to repletion with every solid article of food that reasonable men can wish for,' while 'up yonder wide and splendid staircase . . . you will find a noble coffee-room, private sitting-rooms, &c., (with bedrooms on the other side of the Line,) in fact, all the appurtenances of a first-rate family hotel, nearly every window of which commands magnificent views of the Wiltshire and Berkshire scenery; and should any of our gentleman fellow-passengers desire the luxury of the fragrant cigar, which either on the platforms or the carriages is 'Bann'd and barr'd, forbidden fare,' he may indulge therein to his heart's content in the cheerful covered gallery which runs above and across the line, uniting the two platforms.'

One gets the strong impression that George Measom must have been plied with a free meal or two by Mr Phillips to produce this tribute! Certainly, he can have been no smoker; true followers of the weed would strongly resent having to go for their puff on the overhead footbridge, however covered or "cheerful", while their companions were able to relax in first class comfort downstairs.

For all the tales of pristine maidens, lightning service and bounteous banbury-cakes and ale, railway refreshment in general had by the 1860s become something of a byword for the darker side of things – the awful coffee, the depressing atmosphere and the unsmiling attendants.

It only needed an established author to take up his pen on the theme, and in 1866 Charles Dickens published his short story *Mugby Junction*, a place he was to make famous for its haunted signalbox. Also well-known (though often misquoted) are the more worldly horrors of the Down Refreshment Room there, 'what's proudest boast is, that it never yet refreshed a mortal being.' The following scene from the famous novelist's story takes place 'at past three o'clock of a tempestuous morning'. A belated traveller at Mugby is questioning "Lamps", the only member of the station staff to be found:

'Is there any hotel or tavern here?'
'Not exactly here, sir. There *is* a Refreshment Room here, but . . .'
"Lamps", with a mighty serious look, gave his head a warning roll that plainly added '. . . but it's a blessed circumstance for you that it's not open.'
'You couldn't recommend it, I see, if it was available?'
'Ask your pardon, Sir? If it was—?'
'Open?'
'It ain't my place, as a paid servant of the company, to give my opinion on any of the company's toepics' – he pronounced it more like toothpicks – 'beyond lamp-ile and cottons,' returned "Lamps" in a confidential tone; 'but speaking as a man I wouldn't recommend my father (if he was to come to life again) to go and try how he'd be treated at the Refreshment Room. Not speaking as a man. No; I would *not*.'

And soon, in this story, the reader is introduced to one of the boys who works at this forbidding place, standing as he is by 'a metallic object that's at times the tea-urn and at times the soup tureen: next time you stop in a hurry at Mugby, for anything to drink, you take particular notice that he'll try to seem not to hear you, that he'll appear in an absent manner to survey the Line through a transparent medium composed of your head and body, and that he won't serve you as long as you can possibly bear it. That's me.'

This was the hardest side-swipe at refreshment rooms that Dickens was to take, by by no means the only one. One wonders what poor Mrs Hibbert, the former paragon of Wolverton, who obviously strove very hard for better standards, made of it – especially as she must, like many, have identified Mugby Junction with Rugby, which is on the same line as Wolverton and not that many miles away!

Yet another writer to have a go at railway refreshments was the novelist Anthony Trollope. Here is a passage from *He Knew He was Right*, published in 1868:

'The real disgrace of England is the railway sandwich, – that whited sepulchre, fair enough outside, but so meagre, poor, and spiritless within, such a thing of shreds and parings, with a dab of food, telling us that the poor bone whence it was scraped had been made utterly bare before it was sent into the kitchen for the soup pot.'

So the refreshment outlook for the railway traveller, as the second half of the nineteenth century came around, was firmly set at 'Gloomy'. It was onto this scene of draughty, barn-like rooms, meagre food and worse service that there stepped in the year 1863 two entrepreneurs by the name of Spiers and Pond, who, in the words of a press report of the times, 'had come from Melbourne to improve our railway refreshment facilities'.

This statement, like many press reports, was dramatic but a trifle over-stated. Felix Spiers and Christopher Pond had emigrated separately to Australia in their youth, and met up when Spiers was running the Cafe de Paris in Melbourne. Together they formed a partnership to operate the catering for the Melbourne & Ballarat Railway; this rapidly became a success, and other contracts followed. Then, knowing of the far greater spread of railways back in the Old Country, and hearing no doubt of the dire state of the catering business thereon, they decided to return together and try their luck.

The pair were quickly successful and in 1863 they landed a contract with what today seems an unlikely customer – the Metropolitan Railway in London. However, 1863 was the year of the opening of this, the world's first underground railway, and not only did this guarantee Spiers and Pond considerable exposure and publicity, but it took place at a time when eating houses in central London were by no means as prolific as they were later to become. Spiers and Pond's first buffet was at Farringdon Street, at what at its opening was the eastern terminus of the line, and they soon had a dozen or so in the dark and smoky environs of London's Metropolitan and District Railways. In 1864 they landed the catering contract with the London, Chatham & Dover Railway, opening a refreshment and dining room at London's Victoria station, described by *The Standard* as possessing 'every convenience for supplying the travellers with chops, steaks, tea and coffee at the shortest possible notice and that, too, in a style fit for a nobleman.' A long way indeed from Mugby Junction.

It was not long before this enterprising duo began to turn their thoughts towards a new challenge – the provision of food and drink to be eaten on a moving train. We shall deal with their lunch-baskets, for such was their idea, in a later chapter, but several years were to go before this scheme became a reality. Meantime, other moves were afoot.

2
The Coming of the Cars

The idea of having a moving refreshment room as part of a train had come to the minds of some as early as 1845. Prompted by the infamous rush to swill down red-hot liquid in the few minutes' station time allowed, *Punch* in that year commented:

"The Smoking Saloon on the Eastern Counties is only the first which it is intended to bestow upon travellers by railway. It is in contemplation to run a refreshment room with every train, so that people will have time allowed them to eat the articles sold, instead of being restricted as at present to the privilege of payment . . . It has been suggested that there might be kept and sold at all the refreshment rooms, a preparation similar to that which enabled a certain Monsieur Chabert some years ago to swallow melted lead without any inconvenience . . . the most feasible scheme is, however, a portable refreshment room, one of which should travel with every train."

Although nothing came of these proposals at the time, the idea must have remained alive, for in 1846 we find the *Bristol Gazette* propounding:

"The invention consists in the construction of some newly-formed carriages, so as to constitute a sort of travelling caffe, (*sic*) or railway restaurant, to be placed in the rear of the carriages, which are to be so constructed as to open into one another to an extent, enabling waiters to travel along the train and relieve the *ennui*, so inseparable from railway travelling, by supplies from a locomotive larder at the other end.

'A bill of fare, showing what the refectory contains, is to be posted in each carriage; so that passengers, first, second, and third, may at any time stay the rage of hunger. Bells are to be at the command of the passengers to announce their wants to the waiter, who will travel to them along a narrow passage alongside the interior of the carriages constructed for the purpose. Should the proposed plan be adopted, railway travelling may be ranked among the beatitudes.'

History was to let more than three decades roll by before a part of this plan – the 'travelling caffe' – became reality, and several years more before the other part, corridor trains, allowed the full possibilities to be exploited. Until then, passengers were fated to spend many a long journey bored, cramped, hungry, thirsty, unable to stretch their legs for hours at a time or even go to the toilet. No wonder that the more imaginative began dreaming of 'locomotive larders'!

It was dreams of this kind, amid the prevailing discomfort, that had prompted the American pioneer George Mortimer Pullman as far back as 1859 to turn his attention to creature comforts on board trains. Starting with sleeping cars – an absolute necessity on the great distance traversed by American railroads – Pullman had next introduced day saloons. Then in 1868, on the Chicago & Alton Railroad, he followed this with the world's first dining car, which he named *Delmonico* after a famous New York restaurant. News of these developments quickly crossed the Atlantic, and found a particularly receptive listener in James Allport, General Manager of the Midland Railway.

The Midland had already earned a reputation for making rather more effort than most to look after the comfort of its passengers as much as the speed of its trains. Its station refreshment rooms, for example, had a name for being quite passable where most of the rest were awful, while in 1872 it became the first British railway to allow third class passengers onto all its trains, instead of herding them together on special services with the slowest schedules, the least reliable locomotives, and the most primitive rolling stock. That same year, Allport determined to go to America to see Pullman's carriages for himself, with a view to introducing this luxury form of travel on his own line.

Allport returned full of enthusiasm and determined to press ahead with all speed, and in February 1873 a 15-year agreement was signed with the Pullman Palace Car Company. This arranged for Pullman cars to be built in knocked-down form at its workshops in Detroit, shipped to Britain and assembled at the Midland Railway's Works in Derby. The cars were to be manned exclusively by Pullman's own stewards, with a Pullman supplementary fare charged to customers. Pullman himself was supremely confident of the success of this venture in England –

so much so, that he agreed to bear all the costs of construction, shipment and operation for the 15-year period, without any charge to the Midland Railway itself. Income from the supplementary charge would be sufficient to fund most of the costs, and the rest would be carried as what is known today as a loss-leader. Interestingly, the orders placed were for sleeping and parlour cars, but not for any dining vehicles.

Shipment and construction began at once, and by 21 March 1874 the first three vehicles – two sleepers and a saloon – were ready for a demonstration trip for Press and public, which was to run from St Pancras to Bedford and back. Despite the lack of a dining car, it was felt the occasion warranted something for the inner man; a cold lunch was therefore pre-prepared and served on board. The caterers brought in for this historic occasion – the first-ever meal to be provided on a British train – were none other than those luminaries of the infant London Underground, Messrs Spiers & Pond.

This trip was hailed as a considerable success, and the decision to press ahead with further Pullman cars was confirmed, but for one reason or another the Midland Railway directors still took no step to include any catering vehicles in its Pullman plans, nor indeed to further the idea of on-train dining. This was still the case in 1878 when a private party chartered a special train from St Pancras to Wick, in the far north of Scotland, and back. This party rode and slept in Pullman cars, but as a hot meal service was also called for, a luggage van was fitted out as a kitchen and the meals served into the Pullman parlour car – the first meal to be both cooked and served on a British train. A second luggage van was fitted out as a bathroom, complete with bath.

By this time the Pullman Car Company was eager for new British routes on which to expand, making use of its construction shops at Derby, where a Pullman-appointed manager and staff were now installed. A willing partner for new ventures had been found in the Great Northern Railway, with its busy route from King's Cross to the North, and late in 1875 this line had taken delivery of two Pullman sleepers, named *Ocean* and *Ohio*, which went into service on the journey between King's Cross and Manchester (London Road) via Sheffield. More negotiations followed, during which Henry Oakley, General Manager of the Great Northern, addressed his board as follows:

'I submit herewith a proposal from the Pullman Palace Company to supply us with a day car for our ten o'clock "Scotch Express" which they will fit up, if we like, with accommodation for refreshments so that travellers can obtain foods, etc, on the journey after the fashion of the dining-room saloons on the American Railways'.

Pullman was also offering Oakley the same generous no-risk financing already taken up by Allport on the Midland. Oakley's board duly accepted these proposals, and in 1878 the sleeper *Ohio* was returned to the Pullman Shops at Derby. Late the following summer it emerged, now named *Prince of Wales*, as Britain's first dining car.

There was at least one trial run with this vehicle, to which outsiders were not invited, but any resulting modifications must have been quickly completed, for on Saturday 18 October 1879 the Great Northern organised another demonstration run from King's Cross to Peterborough and back, this time with invited dignitaries and journalists. As Oakley reported to his board: 'A very good dinner was cooked in the car and served much to the satisfaction of all. Mr Tennant, MP, our Director, accompanied the trip down, but left us at Peterborough where Sir Andrew Fairbairn, who was accidentally coming up, joined us on the return journey'. For this journey the Pullman Comapny appointed its first restaurant car conductor in Britain, one James Bower, a native of Portsmouth, who had run away to sea at the age of 14 and eventually fetched up in Chicago. There he had found employment on Pullman's newly-established dining cars, and had later returned to England with George Pullman himself to initiate the services on the Midland Railway. This connection between the sea and the dining car, as we shall see, was to set a precedent that exists to this day.

The meal was a hot one and, according to a press report of the time, was 'capably cooked and well served. The speed of the train was at one time over 60 miles an hour, and the brakes were applied more than once ... no unpleasant movement of the dishes was made, neither the waiter not the boy in buttons tumbled over, and very little of the wine jumped out of the glasses'.

So satisfactory was this demonstration trip that Oakley recommended to his board that public service should begin as soon as possible. The route finally selected was between King's Cross and Leeds, and on Saturday 1 November 1879 *Prince of*

THE FIRST DINING SALOON. G.N.R. 1879

The scene at King's Cross in 1879, with the GNR's Pullman diner, *Prince of Wales*. The artist in this 1920s cigarette card has used a similar but later vehicle as his model; *Prince of Wales* never had the vestibule connection shown here. *Author's collection.*

Wales went into service on the 10.00am Up from Leeds Central, due into London King's Cross at 2.00pm, returning north at 5.30pm, due back into Leeds at 10.10pm. As the *Illustrated London News* of 22 November that year commented:

'A Leeds man, by this arrangement, may start from home after his usual breakfast, fortify himself with lunch at 1 o'clock, take three clear hours for his business in London, dine comfortably at 6 or 7 o'clock, and get to bed in his own house an hour before midnight. This seems to be just what one should want. Irregular dining hours, beyond all doubt, have shortened the lives of many prosperous and active men of business who were little past middle age. The Pullman company therefore deserve our support in this department of their enterprise.'

One such 'businessman' who appeared to make the most of this civilised timetable was apparently the contract caterer on the *Prince of Wales* himself (for initially the Pullman Car Company sub-contracted the catering, its own man, James Bower, maintaining a supervisory role). This caterer, according to an elderly railwayman, was met in at Leeds each night by his own coach and pair, and made an elegant figure as he took the reins to drive home!

The *Illustrated London News* goes on to describe the *Prince of Wales*:

Steward James Bower serves dinner on the *Prince of Wales*, as shown in the *Illustrated London News* of 22 November 1879.

'It is 52ft in length, 8ft in breadth, and runs upon eight wheels. It comprises a dining-saloon in the middle, a kitchen behind, and a smoking-room in front, with steward's pantry, ladies' dressing room, gentlemen's lavatory, cupboards and stoves. The dining-saloon has six tables, three on each side, as represented in our illustration; there are 10 cosy chairs, large, well-stuffed, and covered with crimson velvet, each revolving on a solid pivot. There are electric bells to summon the attendants, who are the cook, the steward or waiter, and the boy of the smoking-room. The refreshments, including wines, are supplied by Pullman's company at ordinary hotel dinner charges. Any first-class passenger on the line may use this Pullman Car on payment of half-a-crown over and above the ordinary fare for his journey. He may enter or quit the Pullman Car at any station where the train stops, but should give notice beforehand of his intention, lest the train be full'.

This problem of physical access to the dining car was a real one. Corridor trains were still a thing of the future, and although *Prince of Wales* was of thoroughbred American Pullman design with open balconies at either end, the only possible way of reaching it when on the move was from the balcony of a similar vehicle adjacent, and the only similar vehicles on the GNR in those days were sleepers. Furthermore, as the picture shows, the balcony at the kitchen end was given over to a homely scullery area where a junior member of staff peeled the potatoes.

These rather unhelpful culinary surroundings, and the coke stove with which the cook had to wrestle, seemed not to deter the catering crew, for *The Engineer* for 24 October 1879 quotes the menu as 'a choice of dishes . . . including soups, fish, entrees, roast joints, puddings and such for dessert. After dining the passenger may walk into the smoking area to take his coffee and cigar'. But there were problems, which the staff did their best to keep from the passengers – the line out of King's Cross is amply blessed with tunnels, where the down-draught used to blow quantities of smoke and smuts from the stove straight out onto the food, unless the cook was very careful. One imagines the poor man getting as black as the engine crew, and wonders what the hygiene inspectors of today would have made of the scene, or of the drops of oil that used to drip from the oil lamps in the roof onto the food being served!

Pullmans meantime were becoming recognised as the ultimate in rail travel in other parts of Britain. The London, Brighton & South Coast Railway had been running Pullman cars between London and Brighton since 1875, and in December 1881 the LBSCR introduced a complete train consisting of four Pullman cars (all ex-Midland Railway) bestowing on them the fine Victorian names *Louise*, *Beatrice*, *Victoria* and *Maud*. *Beatrice* had had the distinction of being the first railway carriage in the world to be lit by electricity; large accumulators under the vehicle were re-charged at the end of each trip. *Victoria* also had a small pantry and buffet for service of light refreshments and drinks, thus becoming the second catering vehicle in Britain, though hardly on the scale of the *Prince of Wales*. A couple of years later, *Maud* was converted to a proper dining car offering full meals.

This last move was pre-empted by the Midland Railway itself, which rather belatedly concluded that besides assembling and converting Pullman dining cars for others, there was good business to be done in operating them nearer home – in particular on the busy route from St Pancras to Manchester and Liverpool via Leicester and Derby. Two existing parlour cars, *Britannia* and *Leo*, were converted into what the Midland Railway called 'hotel cars' in 1882 and re-named *Windsor* and

The verandah scullery of the *Prince of Wales*. *Illustrated London News.*

Delmonico respectively (the latter after Pullman's original resturant car on the Chicago & Alton Railroad).

The interiors of these two vehicles, each seating 21 diners, were handsomely panelled in mahogany decorated with paintings of fruit and leaves, while liberal use of mirrors enhanced the sense of space. The cooking was done on a coke-fired range that could cater for 40 people and which, according to the trade union journal *The Railway Review*, produced a meal on the trial trip that 'comprised six courses, beginning with soup and ending with dessert, and was prepared as at an hotel.'

The two cars went into service on 10 July 1882, one on the 5.00pm express from London St Pancras to Manchester and Liverpool, the other on the 4.05pm from Liverpool in the reverse direction. On each train, table d'hôte dinner was served at 6.00pm, while for wines, passengers were advised to place orders before departure with the Conductor, who would 'obtain them from the refreshment room.' Apparently these refreshment rooms stocked something more up-market than the ale and stout swigged by the gallon at places like Wolverton! Pressure on space also prompted the company to advise Manchester passengers, joining in the Up direction, to notify the stationmaster at Central Station before 3.00pm, so that seats could be reserved from Liverpool by telegram.

Such then were the beginnings of restaurant cars in Britain – promoted and operated entirely by the Pullman Car Company and its contractors. On the Midland Railway, however, the Board decided in 1883 to purchase the two dining cars outright from Pullman, along with a number of parlour cars, three of which were soon converted into diners for the Leeds and Bradford expresses. This move meant that for the first time diners did not have to pay the 2s 6d (12½p) Pullman supplementary charge, something which had always been a bone of contention; but the vehicles still remained exclusively first-class. The Great Northern Railway purchased its pioneering *Prince of Wales* outright in 1885, replacing the coke range with an oil-gas cooker, dropping the name and replacing it with the humdrum number 2297. *Prince of Wales* had had a lucky escape from serious damage in a fire at Leeds in 1882. It was to survive in service until 1901, by which time other dining cars, with no Pullman ancestry or design, had taken over and built up the service.

The Pullman Car Company went on to build up a fine network of luxury services in this country, and in Europe. Their story has been ably told elsewhere, with all its glamour and great names; and its more unexpected developments, too, such as the two refreshment cars that from 1910 to 1939 provided a luxury service to commuters on that most unlikely of Pullman domains – the Metropolitan line from Aldgate and Liverpool Street to Aylesbury on the London Underground. We shall meet Pullman again later in our story, when the great changes took place after the 1948 Nationalisation.

So far, all the British diners had been thoroughbred American vehicles. It was the London & North Western Railway, with its great trunk route between Liverpool, Manchester and London Euston, that was to build the first dining cars to a truly British design. Operated in pairs gangwayed together, these vehicles were still not gangwayed to the rest of the train, and they were still first class only. The first pair went into service in March 1889 between Euston and Manchester, followed a month later by another between Euston and Liverpool. These dining cars looked somewhat home-spun by Pullman standards, especially from the outside where the small, widely-spaced windows gave them the appearance (according to a contemporary account) of 'Russian Carriages'. Inside, however, the furnishing was in the elaborately patterned style of the day, and the seats were still very roomy, with only one each side of the central corridor.

At this early stage in the dining car story, the economics of the business were somewhat uncertain. That great institution, the Great Western Railway, still hampered by that confounded compulsory coffee stop at Swindon, was keenly watching the fortunes of others in the dining car world. So it was probably with a fair amount of *schadenfreude* that the Great Western Committee listened to a report of six months' experience on the newly-born LNWR dining car services. That report, for the six months ended 31 December 1890, revealed that on the northbound Euston to Manchester and Liverpool services 8,815 passengers travelled, of whom all but 31 partook of full meals. Receipts were £2,787, yet they still fell short of costs by some £30 – and that excluded the costs of construction, maintenance and gas for cooking and lighting. These figures show that an average of no more than 24 passengers dined on each train. There was every indication of demand being much higher than that, so the lack of gangways into the rest of the train, which would allow more than one sitting per journey, was clearly handicapping the business badly.

The next step forward was to bring the benefits of the dining car to the humble third class passenger. This radical move came in 1891, and it came, not on one of the great trunk lines with a London terminus, but on the Great Eastern Railway's cross-country boat train running between Harwich and York. The coaches used were a three-car set of six-wheeled vehicles gangwayed together, with a kitchen car in the centre; in one of the flanking vehicles, a third class saloon, was one compartment fitted with a dining table for six. Fresh from the rigours of a steerage passage on the Harwich ferry, the third class travellers must have swooned at the sight of such beneficence.

This pioneering outfit was still separated from the rest of the train, and people of all classes still had to wait for station stops to get into or out of the restaurant cars. The honours for the first fully gangwayed train went in 1892 to the Great Western Railway, which brought in just such a train on its Padding-Birkenhead service, followed the next year by others on the South Wales and West Country trains. The snag with these trains, though, was that they still contained no restaurant car. So as far as the corridors went, as one wag put it at the time, 'The paths of glory led but to the luggage van.'

These developments were not lost on the major companies with the London to Scotland routes, and in July 1893 the East Coast companies – Great Northern, North Eastern and North British – introduced dining for both first and third class on their crack 12 noon King's Cross to Edinburgh service. But the West Coast companies, the London & North Western and the Caledonian, went one better on the 2.00pm Euston to Glasgow, for not only was there dining for all, but it was also served in a fully-gangwayed train. At long last one of the major companies had 'got it all together,' and so famous did this train quickly become that the 2.00pm departure from Euston was known as 'The Corridor' right up to World War II, by which time all the other expresses had long had corridors as well. In those days, though, corridors took a bit of getting used to by railwaymen and passengers alike, and there were many loud complaints about intrusions into privacy as people traipsed to and from the dining car.

Another major competitor in the fight for Scottish traffic was the Midland Railway, with its ally the Glasgow & South Western Railway. Ever jealous of its reputation for looking after its passengers, the Midland was operating very superior dining rooms at Normanton, near Leeds, where its Scottish expresses stopped for lunch, and it had a head start in the comfort stakes with its pioneering Pullman cars. But by the 1890s, it was rebuilds of these same early Pullmans that were still feeding and watering the Midland's passengers. Comfortable and solid enough, they were all getting rather long in the tooth and were wont to be reported to the carriage examiners as 'weaving' when at speed. Chairman James Allport therefore commissioned from T. G. Clayton, his chief carriage designer, a very handsome new 12-wheel kitchen restaurant car, which appeared from Derby in 1892, and which was to set the pace in dining car design for years to come. This splendid vehicle boasted a double oven gas cooker, a boiler and a 'fridge' – though with the state of technology at the time, this was probably a zinc-lined receptacle for wet ice.

The Midland – G&SW main line also traversed, between Settle and Carlisle, a route of scenic beauty unrivalled by any of the others. In 1894 the best train of the day was the 1.30pm from London St Pancras to Glasgow St Enoch, and a journey on it was an experience satisfying to body and soul alike. Immediately on leaving St Pancras, luncheon would be served. After a run through the pleasant East Midland shires, afternoon tea would be available between 4.30pm and 6.00pm, taking passengers' minds off the less scenic delights of South Yorkshire heavy industry. This repast would cost 9d (4p) for first class passengers, but only 6d (2½p) for the humble third class. Then, as the train headed up that magnificent route over the Pennine fells in the gathering evening a full table d'hôte dinner would be served in Thomas Clayton's handsome new dining cars. Luxury indeed!

The attractions of this journey, and the trains that ran it, boosted Midland Railway business enormously and far more people wanted to dine than there were seats available. Without inter-coach gangways the concept of 'fluid dining' – doing as many sittings as necessary in the restaurant car – was still not practicable, and thoughts turned instead to trying to increase the size of the dining cars themselves, to take more seats. In September 1895 a carriage was fitted up with templates on each

side, 3in wide, increasing its width from 8ft 6in to 9ft 0in, and
this coach was taken on a round trip from Derby to Stockport,
Liverpool, Manchester and back to see what would happen.
What happened was that the templates were knocked off by the
tight clearances in several tunnels, and by a coach standing on
an adjacent track in Liverpool station. Clearly there was no
room for expansion that way, and so it was that by 1898 the
Midland followed the lead of the West Coast companies and
began gangwaying its dining vehicles into the rest of the train
although it was into the new century before corridor trains
became widely used on the Midland. The fluid dining system
thus established was certainly good for business, but it ended the
leisurely note which had previously characterised meal service,
and it called for considerable re-thinking among restaurant car
management and staff.

The directors of the Great Western Railway, whose services in
mid 1890s still bore the handicap of that compulsory coffee stop
at Swindon, had remained, until the advent of through
gangways and fluid dining as introduced on the East and West
Coast routes, sceptical about the economics of restaurant cars.
But it must have been bowing to the inevitable when, at the end
of 1895, the directors decided that the future of long-distance
services lay in cutting out intermediate stops, catering instead
on the trains themselves. That meant grasping the Swindon
nettle, and the final impetus for this came from the operating
department, which was becoming very vociferous about
congestion in the station and pressure on platform space caused
by the long stops there. As we have seen, it cost the company
£100,000 to buy out the contract and get rid of the compulsory
stop once and for all. Thus freed, the Great Western in May 1896
put into service its first three dining cars, on the South Wales
and West Country routes, adding a fourth the following year.
The company was not immediately ready to undertake its own
catering, and for the first eighteen months the job was
contracted out to the firm of Browning & Wesley, which ran
many of the GWR station refreshment rooms, including the ones
at Paddington where the trains were victualled.

South of the Thames, shorter distances meant less demand for
dining car services, and for a long while these were restricted to
the Pullman services which the London, Brighton & South
Coast Railway had began in 1882. However, in 1891 the South

Eastern Railway, keen to compete with LBSCR for the Hastings traffic, assembled at its Ashford Works a number of American-built 'Mock Pullman' vehicles, with pantries for limited meal service. In 1897 the SER introduced a second luxury service with the 'Folkestone car train'. A decade later these vehicles, along with the service they offered, were taken over by Pullman proper. On the London & South Western Railway out of Waterloo, no dining cars appeared until 1901, by which time West Country travellers considered them long overdue. The LSWR had already appointed as its station caterers none other than Spiers & Pond, and had no hesitation in appointing the same firm to run the on-train services too. Between them, Pullman and Spiers & Pond now ran all the train catering on the companies that later formed the Southern Railway.

In 1899, a new railway and a new style of catering approached London from the North. The provincial Manchester, Sheffield & Lincolnshire Railway company (rudely dubbed the 'Money Sunk & Lost' after its initials) opened its new main line to London Marylebone via Leicester, Rugby and Aylesbury, and having taken the imposing title Great Central Railway, announced that there would be a buffet car on 'every express train.'

The inside of these buffet cars looked every inch a miniature pub on wheels. Furnished in the heavily-decorated style of late Victorian days, they sported appropriate pictures on the walls while across a corner stood an elegant and very substantial mahogany bar. The series of wall pictures – 'Gentlemen Smoking' for example – is still reproduced for the modern trade, while anyone visiting the bar at the Great Central's Marylebone terminus – which survives as a genuine Victorian bar to this day – would at once recognise the design and fittings in the buffet cars as being from the same stable.

But the travelling public, ever a conservative body, was not ready for such innovations. In the case of the Great Central they were Conservative with a capital C as well, for the best business of the line came from the landed gentry of the East Midland hunting shires. The gentry looked at the new-fangled buffet cars, and did not like what it saw. Bars were associated with sordid public houses, and the gentry did not patronise such places. One did not know with whom one might have to rub shoulders! The *hoi-polloi*, too, seemed to feel uncomfortable about using the cars, so in 1907–8 these pioneering vehicles

The Great Central Railway's handsome buffet car, built for the opening of its main line to London Marylebone in 1899. *BBC Hulton Picture Library.*

were converted to orthodox restaurant cars. A quarter of a century was to go by before buffet cars would be tried again, by which time life in Britain had changed out of all recognition.

So it was that by the turn of the century, 'dinner in the diner' was an established habit for all classes on most of Britain's main lines. A particular landmark came on 1 August 1900, when the East Coast companies finally cut out the famous luncheon stop at York on the Flying Scotsman, which had been a feature of life for some 40 years. The standard of dining car accommodation varied, but that heavy and ornate decoration, so typical of late Victorian and Edwardian days, dominated the scene in most vehicles. Particular plaudits for design went to the Great Northern Railway's Doncaster-built first class cars of 1907, decorated in the 'Adam style,' with wall and ceiling pannellings all in white, the London firm of Waring having been called in as

A GNR diner of about 1898 – one of the cars that spelt the end of the luncheon stop on the Flying Scotsman. *British Rail.*

interior designer. So successful indeed was this move that Nigel Gresley, the GNR's Chief Mechanical Engineer, thenceforward always used a commercial interior designer for his prestige rolling stock.

At the other end of the scale were light refreshment facilities such as those operated by the GWR on its Milford Haven boat trains in the early 1900s. Here, the 'facility' took up the space of just two compartments; one attendant had to prepare and serve anywhere in the train hot beverages and snacks, using just one household stove. 'Market penetration,' it is safe to say, must have been low!

In July 1902, the theatre critic Austin Brereton conducted a survey of the dining car services of the day, company by company, in *Transport* magazine. The survey showed most of the main line services from London well covered, but rather scant provision for cross-country services – a situation dictated by the pattern of heaviest passenger travel, and not unlike that prevailing today. Prices of meals were more or less uniform throughout the country: luncheon would cost 2s 6d (12½p) for all passengers, whereas dinner would set the first class traveller back 3s 6d (17½p), but his third class companion only 3s 0d (15p).

Top of the bill for quality, in Brereton's eyes, came the

Midland Railway, whose reputation under its enterprising hotels and catering manager William Towle continued to hold good:

> 'In every respect – selection of food, its quality and cooking and the charge made for it – the Midland Railway have left nothing to be desired, and be it remembered, they pay equal attention to the wants of the third class passenger as to those of the first – thereby setting a high standard. Again, the Midland wine list is very extensive – so that one's choice is not restricted, as is so often the case, to a stock wine – and the price asked is very reasonable indeed. Another good point about the Midland is that you can obtain, when the ordinary meals are not being served, other refreshments; varying from tea and coffee with toast and butter for 9d, up to the chop or steak with fried potatoes, bread, butter etc, and tea or coffee for half-a-crown'.

This lighter meal obviously filled a need that some of the other railways were slow to meet. One big company operated a special arrangement for some of its less moneyed clients:

> 'The Great Northern, be it noted, makes special arrangements whereby emigrants are supplied with a meat sandwich, bread and butter and coffee, for sixpence, while our Jack Tars and Tommy Atkinses can obtain a good meal of cold meat, bread and beer, for the humble shilling.'

Thus it was that Englishmen went forth to fight the Boer War, or to start a new life in Australia, fortified by cheap GNR sandwiches!

Among the provincial services, Brereton picked out for special mention the North Eastern Railway's first class refreshment car, operated between Scarborough and Leeds and vice-versa 'for the benefit of businessmen'. This was one of the original ex-Midland Railway Pullman cars that went to the North Eastern during the 1880s. He mentions, too, the joint service operated by the North Eastern, Great Central, Great Western, and London & South Western Railways, 7.05 am Newcastle to Bournemouth, serving breakfast and lunch, and 10.47am Bournemouth to Newcastle, serving lunch and dinner. This eleven-hour cross-country service, new to the railway timetable that year, is described as 'one of the most remarkable trains in existence,' and so indeed, in its day, it was.

Then there was the Lancashire & Yorkshire Railway, which ran 'breakfast and dining cars between Fleetwood, Manchester,

Bradford and Leeds, a convenience very greatly appreciated by passengers travelling between England and Ireland by the Fleetwood route.' (It was this service that for a time sported a remarkable L&YR catering car with a six-wheel bogie at one end and a four-wheel one at the other, and a roof which was part clerestory and part elliptical). The Glasgow & South Western Railway had a car on the 6.30am Carlisle to Glasgow St Enoch and the 5.30pm back. The Highland Railway as yet operated no dining cars, but did considerable business with the 'Kingussie' breakfast basket, of which no fewer than 10,000 were prepared and handed into the trains in the course of a season.

Without a doubt, the institution of the dining car had come to be a much-looked-for part of every railway company's service. But it is plain from Brereton's piece that the London & North Western company in particular, which through its constituent, the London & Birmingham, had pioneered railway catering, was still living down its 'Mugby Junction' catering reputation – at the same time, this railway had much the most extensive restaurant car service. By the summer of 1906 it was operating

LNWR dining car stewards pose alongside their vehicle, No 483, in this turn of the century view. *British Rail.*

no fewer than 100 restaurant cars and employed 280 staff to work them; in the off-season this dwindled to 87 vehicles in use per weekday, with 256 men employed. On the morning trains from Scotland four relays of luncheon were frequently served, with Crewe often passed before the last sitting was called. A contemporary account considered that this demand for full meals rendered an à-la-carte service of fish, chop or steaks, impossible. Certainly the Midland Railway, praised particularly by Austin Brereton for providing just such a service outside peak times, is unlikely to have faced four full sittings of luncheon on its southbound Scottish Expresses.

This overstrain on L&NW resources was now beginning to show itself in dissatisfaction among both public and staff. A typical letter in the *Liverpool Mercury* of 25 July 1904 complains of the service on the 5.30pm from Euston; the writer got to the station a quarter of an hour before the train started, but was unable to find a seat in the dining cars, all having previously been booked. There was only one sitting of dinner during this journey. 'May I suggest,' he concluded, 'that, as the trains are corridor ones, a special coach should be fitted up as a buffet, so that light refreshments could be obtained at any time while en route?' This correspondent had a point, for the LNWR served a much less rarified passenger catchment area than the genteel shires of the Great Central, whose buffet cars were not exactly pulling the crowds – lines such as the LNWR might have made a go of buffets where others could not.

Shortage of accommodation was not the only cause of complaint. The price of meals, despite Austin Brereton's well-phrased 'puff,' was a bone of contention among passengers, most of whom knew or cared little about the costs of providing meals on trains – something that remains just as much of a problem 80 years on. There were other grumbles, too; the quality of the food and – something which one no longer hears – the miniscule size of the portions.

All these things surfaced in an article in *The Tourist* magazine for July 1903, which began by asserting with cheerful ignorance that 'it is just as easy to prepare and serve as good a meal *en route*, and at popular prices, as in ordinary usage.' The wonder of 20 years before had quickly become the commonplace of the Edwardian era; even so, this was a particularly block-headed assertion, no doubt from a writer light-years away from the realities of serving four consecutive full sittings of lunch on that Scotch express!

One does however develop a little more sympathy with him as the menus for the two journeys unfold. A 2s 6d (12½p) lunch on the London & North Western began with boiled haddock and parsley sauce, 'the fish full of bones, small and watery, the grumbler was fortunate (*sic*) enough to secure the fag end of the tail, certainly not appetising.' Then came Roast Beef, Pressed Beef or Ham – the latter the writer's party 'regretted insulting their gastric juices with.' The vegetables were cabbage and potatoes, 'so beautifully messed up that we passed the dish,' while salad was on the menu but was not forthcoming. Apple Pie and custard were 'passable.'

This sounds like the worst of traditional British cooking, which for very many years was by no means confined to the railways. The much-vaunted Midland Railway came off no better, which cannot have pleased hotel and catering manager William Towle. At a 3s 0d (15p) dinner, the soup – Crème Chasseur – was excellent but the quantity tiny. 'No doubt,' says the writer, 'the company would excuse themselves on the grounds of the oscillation of the train – certainly the bottom of the plate was hardly covered, and this is a general fault.' For fish came halibut and caper sauce, 'about two square inches,' while the main courses was curry of chicken – described as 'Skin and Grief!' – with 'the usual imperfectly drained vegetables.' And finally, Apple Dumpling, '*half a small one each.*' Oh dear! As the writer concluded, the only way to feed even a moderate appetite was to have recourse to the 'conspicuous and questionable taste of a double go all round.'

Such complaints notwithstanding, business continued to build steadily, and not surprisingly the staff attempted to catch the wind. The trade union *Railway Review* of 11 September 1908 alleged:

'In 1907 no less than 831,324 meals were served on the L&NWR, an increase of nearly 10% in one year alone. We shall be surprised if the men on the cars are not able to convince Mr Waters – their chief – that there is unanswerable case for a substantial increase in their present meagre pay.'

Improvements in pay may have been forthcoming only slowly, but improvements in conditions for passengers continued apace.

The well-appointed table and padded seats of a GWR diner just before the Great War. The 2s 6d (12½p) supper menu is headed 'Guaranteed excursion, Tredegar to London, February 14th 1914' while the notice on the panelling warns passengers that seats must be vacated immediately the meal is finished. *British Rail/Oxford Publishing Co.*

Most cars were by now luxuriously fitted and upholstered, well-lighted, warmed and ventilated, while several, according to the *Railway Times*, were fitted with an apparatus for the supply of ozone. This, according to the season of the year, could be passed into the car in the form of either hot or cold air. In summer this device, together with revolving electric fans, was found to keep the temperature 'much lower than was possible by the ordinary means of ventilation,' while in winter 'the more equal distribution of heat, entering from the roof, gave a sense of extreme comfort and general warmth.'

Ozone or no, such a sense of well-being permeated all those who experienced restaurant car travel at its best. This well-being blended with an aura of romance that was very powerful in the old days – and indeed is still powerful today. To sum-up the glow of that Edwardian heyday, here in full is an account of a journey as it appeared in the *Manchester Evening Chronicle* of 7 November 1904. No doubt a well-planned public relations exercise lay behind it. It worked.

'Euston looked quite gay under the autumn sun as we took our reserved places in a saloon of the 8.30 express to the far north. Lounging in a cosy corner upon a seat which is very like an arm chair, and looking down this splendid carriage of the L&NWR Company, you can almost imagine you are in the coffee room of a first-class hotel. Electric lights gleam in the ornamental roof; a globe is fixed over each seat so that we may read without straining the eyes; the woodwork is richly carved, the upholstery luxurious; an electric bell is at our side; the air is pleasantly warmed, and a circular fan keeps the supply pure.

'The little table before us is laid for breakfast, and as we glide through the suburbs of the Metropolis waiters in neat uniforms appear with coffee, fish, eggs, bacon, cutlets, toast, and so on. We are travelling at certainly fifty miles an hour, but so good is the permanent way, and so well-balanced the coach, that not a drop of coffee splashes over into the saucer. When the marmalade stage is reached we are racing through the open country, between green fields dotted with farms and queer-shaped barns, and sprinkled with sheep and cows, past canals and slow-moving barges, through tiny towns with their pretty churches. Lakes and woods flash by as we contentedly settle down to read the morning's news or to chat with our neighbour on the other side of the table. The train moves not only smoothly but with very little noise, and even as we plunge into a cutting with high chalk walls I can hear an Irish gentleman at the far end of the saloon discussing wages with a Lancashire mill-owner. A brief halt at Rugby prompts a legal light from Wales to tell of his days at the famous school, and the topic is so entertaining that he has not finished when we reach Crewe. London Road (Manchester) is reached not ten seconds behind the advertised time, and I have three and a half clear hours for business and pleasure.

'If the journey from the South had been pleasant, coming back from the north was more enjoyable still. In the open spaces between Manchester and Stockport innumerable young men, mainly attired in shirts of brightest hue, are playing football with science and vigour, while at Cheadle Hulme the pastime is lacrosse, and still further out it is hockey. The steward brings refreshing tea, and from the wide windows I marvel at the golden sunset which makes one think that paradise is just the other side of Alderley Edge. The western sky is aglow with rich tints, while above are the darkening clouds of the coming night. Even the smoke-pall hanging over Crewe cannot shut out the golden streak, and the busy town has quite a romantic appearance in the blurring half-light.

'Gradually the landscape fades from view and is wrapped in darkness, but our carriage is a blaze of light, so that we scarce notice the rush through the night. The waiter, who appears with soup, says that we are doing sixty miles an hour, though it is difficult to realise it. In the best West-end restaurant style fish, joint, poultry, sweets, cheese, dessert, coffee and liqueurs are produced in a magic kind of way from an absurdly small room at the end of the carriage. Having eaten of the fat of the line, we snuggle down with sweet content in our hearts, and cigars in our mouths, until twinkling lights, dimly seen on either side, warns us that London is nigh.

'But even now we are to have another demonstration of the possibilities of this hotel on wheels. A passenger awakes, notes that we are nearing Willesden Junction, calls for writing paper and, without in any way being troubled by the motion of the train, pens a note which is handed to an attendant for despatch per the post. A wash and brush-up finds us once again at Euston, with a long line of porters standing as a guard of honour. Walking down the platform I can scarce believe I have travelled three hundred and sixty-eight miles, for I do not feel in the least weary, and I am more fresh than after many a five mile journey across London.'

Twenty-five years after that first run by the *Prince of Wales* on the Great Northern line, the golden age of restaurant car travel had well and truly arrived.

3
Refreshment Rendezvous

While railway passengers were making themselves comfortable in more and better restaurant cars, enjoying a service imbued with some style and romance, the story on stations was taking a rather different turn. We left our travellers at the end of Chapter 1 in a gloomy world summed up by the *Railway Traveller's Handybook*, first published in 1862, which urged its readers to be quick and concise in the refreshment room throng, not to waste words – 'never mind "a basin of", but simply utter the monosyllable "soup" ' – and to call out orders in a loud voice.

This was the world in which Felix Spiers and Christopher Pond, newly returned from Australia, made their first British catering ventures. By 1864 these two entrepreneurs had established a firm foothold in London and on the Dover run. They had also entered the world of railway hotels, and were soon to inaugurate a lunch-basket service, both of which we shall come to later. Meantime, they set about consolidating and expanding their contracts in refreshment rooms. Through the late nineteenth century their empire was to grow until, beside its London interests, it covered railways as diverse as the South Eastern, London & South Western, Midland, Great Eastern, Manchester, Sheffield & Lincolnshire, Lancashire & Yorkshire, Furness, Cambrian, North British, and Cheshire Lines Committee. No single railway company served quite such varying terrain as rural Dorset on the one hand, and the solid but grimy worth of places like Rotherham Central, in South Yorkshire, on the other – centre of the heaviest of heavy industry.

For good measure, Spiers and Pond began the Silver Grill chain of restaurants, the first opening in 1866 in the arches under Ludgate Hill Station, LC&DR. The firm continued to prosper, and as late as 1929 was still enough of a force to take on the catering at Chiltern Court, the Metropolitan Railway's newly-opened showpiece over Baker Street Station. This massive and handsome building, still a landmark today, included residential flats, offices, with a restaurant and ballroom on the ground floor.

The problem now facing railway management and contractors alike was how to get round the conditions for which refreshment rooms had become notorious. First and foremost this meant the incessant overcrowding, pushing, and barging. Wolverton had shown the way with its very long counter, staffed by its 'seven very young ladies', and in due course extra-long counters began to find their way into other rooms up and down the country. Remember that before the coming of the railways, the inns and refreshment houses of the country generally had no counters at all. To the railways therefore belongs the credit for something that has been an integral part of cafes, and particularly pubs, for what is usually considered time immemorial. No so. The bartender in the Wild West saloon, nervously eyeing the gun-slinging outlaw as he served up his large whisky, had Wolverton, England, to thank for the sixty or so feet of stout timber protecting his bottles and his daughter.

As the rooms began to develop into rather less daunting places to be, some of them, particularly in the more favoured locations, started to become gathering points in their own right. One of these was at Callander in the Scottish Highlands, where the station, already an exchange point for mails, was becoming the centre for road tours in the Trossachs as well as serving nearby hotels. The various horse-drawn coaches engaged in these businesses used to congregate outside the railway refreshment room, which opened onto the road as well as the railway platform. The station building in late Victorian times was a rather colonial-looking wooden structure, and the whole scene had an appearance very much akin to the Wild West, outside the saloon as well as inside.

Unfortunately, heavy drinking was beginning to play a rather larger part in the refreshment room scene than the railway authorities might have liked. Though it brought in good revenue, it added at the same time a cachet of social undesirability to places whose reputation was already far from brilliant. The liquor licensing laws in the mid-nineteenth century were far more lax than those of today; in general, instead of specifying limited hours when a beerhouse might

Saloon Trade: horse-drawn carriages gather outside the refreshment rooms at Callander about 1880, awaiting the next trainload of tourists. *Author's collection.*

open, as now, they merely specified a few limited occasions when it was to be closed. These occasions basically comprised Good Friday, Christmas Day, and 'during the hours of Divine Service on Sundays' (later altered to cover most of Sundays). Even these restrictions were waived if the beerhouse was open 'for the reception of travellers'. In other words, railway refreshment rooms provided a never-ending source of booze to most of the people most of the time, particularly to anyone with the means (honest or otherwise) of identifying himself as a bona-fide traveller.

Francis Head had already regretfully noted that a very large number of bottles of spirits figured among the sales turnover at Wolverton. So strongly did Head feel about this that he opined:

'Considering not only the serious accidents that may occur to individual passengers from intoxication, but the violence and insolence which drunken men may inflict upon travellers of both sexes, whose misfortune it may be to be shut up with them; it would be well for managers of the company . . . peremptorily to forbid, at all

their refreshment rooms, the sale by any of their servants, to the
public, of ardent spirits.'

As the nineteenth century drew towards its end, the evils of
drink became the target of crusades right across the country,
accompanied by a certain amount of tinkering with the licensing
laws. The railways were for the most part eager to swim with the
moral tide, and in November 1906 we find *The Daily Telegraph*
speaking of the Great Eastern facilities at Liverpool Street:

'In striking contrast to the methods of the caterer of ten years back,
the management do their best to push the sale of non-alcoholic
drinks. They do not countenance, and indeed strongly object to their
buffets and refreshment-rooms being turned into drinking-shops or
convivial meeting places.'

But this puritanical attitude was not exactly universal, and
there were still plenty of people prepared to exploit the loopholes,
especially that of being a bona-fide traveller, so as to go drinking
on the Sabbath. Local train services on Sundays were more
intense in those days than now, and a favourite dodge was to buy
a cheap ticket to any station further away than the three miles
demanded by the law, and then booze away the day in one or
both refreshment rooms. A number of hardened characters did
not even bother to buy a ticket if they thought they could get
away with it – for example, if the man at the ticket barrier could
be bribed with a wink, and an inexperienced young member of
staff were on duty behind the bar. One such case in Wigan in
1907, reported on at length in the weekly paper, concerned four
local ne'er-do-wells who bamboozled just such a young
refreshment lady into serving them, by pretending they were
part of a group of travelling actors who were on the station. In
due course the actors went to join their train, leaving behind our
four conspirators, plus a plain-clothes constable who had
unobtrusively joined the group, and who recognised them at
once. The London & North Western Railway was duly
summoned for selling liquor to unauthorised persons out of
hours, but the manageress pleaded that the actors held a
communal ticket, and it was far from clear who that ticket
applied to among the crowd confronting her. Eventually, no
doubt to the smug satisfaction of our four friends, the case was
dismissed.

Tippler's Paradise: the station buffet, like this one at King's Cross in 1903, was once the ideal place to take full advantage of lax licensing laws. *Mary Evans Picture Library*.

Then, as now, the soldiery was very prone to take advantage of railway drinking facilities. One night late in 1906, a trooper was found lying in 'a helpless state of drunkenness' across the pavement in Crewe, and on being taken to the police station was still so helpless that the duty officer felt bound to make further inquiries. Eventually it transpired that the soldier and his four cronies had been discharged from Gosport that morning, where they had no doubt celebrated the fact, and journeyed to Euston Station in London where each purchased a bottle of whisky. They cleared that by Bletchley, at which point they bought three more bottles. By Rugby (just 36 miles further on!) these too were drained dry, so out staggered our heroes again to invest in five more bottles. When at length they arrived at Crewe, in the sober words of the *Crewe Guardian*, 'prisoner and majority of his colleagues were drunk, and he (prisoner) remembered no more.'

Cases like this showed that there was still a long way to go in tightening control of drinking, both on the railways and off. Ironically, it was not until World War I that a national initiative was taken by Prime Minister Lloyd George, who changed the licensing laws in draconian fashion to stop thirsty munitions workers becoming legless on duty and damaging the War effort. These restrictions were organised by a committee that included none other than William Towle, newly retired as hotel and catering supremo of the Midland Railway. Intended as a temporary measure for the duration of hostilities, the changes have in fact never been reversed, and remain substantially unaltered (except in Scotland and in England and Wales with meals) today.

But we run ahead of ourselves. Drinking dens or no, the refreshment room was considered a desirable facility and if a new station were for any reason constructed without one, the community was likely to find ways of filling the gap. At Todmorden for example, on the Lancashire/Yorkshire border, the narrow river valley in which the railway runs provided something of an obstacle, for the cramped station layout left no space for any refreshment room. But in 1865, the landlord of the Queen Hotel across the road obliged by opening one on his first floor, level with the station platforms opposite, and a special passenger footbridge was put up to connect the two buildings.

A major feature of Victorian railway travel was the rigid separation of passengers into first, second and third class, on the station as well as on the train. Three lots of waiting and refreshment rooms were usual on large stations, and at many smaller ones besides; at the famous Swindon hotel and refreshment rooms, third class passengers were indeed completely excluded from the main block.

The lower-class rooms were basic indeed compared to their more up-market counterparts. At Bletchley, then an important junction on the LNWR main line, an old print (unfortunately of very poor quality) shows the third class bar as a small, gloomy basement furnished only with bare wooden benches and table. At Stafford, further north on the same line, the first class room occupied a spacious 1,300sq ft, while the second class, presumably catering for a much greater number of passengers, occupied only 774sq ft. Furthermore, the only way into the ladies' second class waiting room and toilets was through the *gentlemen's* second class waiting room! Such a thing would certainly not have been tolerated by first class passengers. There were also unkind observers, as our *Punch* cartoon shows, who suggested that the food, too, was 'cascaded' down the classes as its freshness diminished – rather after the manner of

BEHIND THE SCENES

Head Barmaid. "These tarts are quite stale, Miss Hunt—
been on the counter for a fortnight! *Would* you mind taking
them into the *second-class* refreshment-room?"

A classic jibe at refreshment-room fare, from *Punch* of 3 December
1881.

passenger rolling stock in the modern age.

The pattern of class distinction began to change when second
class carriages were withdrawn late in the nineteenth century,
and second class station rooms soon followed; it was to be the
1920s before social change made separate refreshment rooms an
outdated concept altogether.

By that time, many railways were already cutting the cake of
custom another way, with rooms offering different menus
instead of serving different classes. The main spur for this had
been the atmosphere of heavy drinking that often prevailed, and
at the larger terminals luncheon rooms and particularly tea
rooms had grown up with an eye to business from ladies and

families. At Liverpool Street in London, the Great Eastern Railway built no fewer than three tea-rooms in the form of Gothic-style 'gazebos' jutting out from the mezzanine walkway. These welcoming rooms, with their quiet atmosphere of tea and buttered toast amid the smoky bustle of the station, became well-known as pleasant places from which to watch the world go by; the *Great Eastern Railway Magazine* for many years ran a diary feature entitled 'From the Tea-room window', the masthead being a woodcut of the distinctive mullions of the Liverpool Street gazebos.

One of these Victorian treasures remains in service today as a very popular bistro; but with the imminent redevelopment of the station, its days are almost certainly numbered. Vanished too is another interesting Great Eastern relic – the Tea Pavilion built on Great Britain's easternmost extremity, Lowestoft Pier, where no doubt the bracing climate ensured good business in the sale of hot beverages. But a luckier fate has befallen two very attractive tea rooms of the former North Eastern Railway, both wooden art nouveau structures designed by William Bell; the one at Hull (1904) is the subject of imaginative plans by the City Council, while that at York (1906) has been excellently restored

William Bell's handsome Tea Room and Cafe built for the NER at York Station in 1906, and now the Rail Riders' Club HQ. *Crown Copyright. National Railway Museum, York.*

and now houses a centre for Rail Riders, the children's travel club.

Amid all the various kinds of refreshment room, which between them took up a great deal of valuable space on stations, one particular style of rendezvous stood out as synonymous with long-distance travel for a generation and more: the great dining-rooms that served as halfway stopping-points on the long trek between London and Scotland. We have already seen how the restaurant car slowly began to meet this market in the 1890s, but through services had already been running for over 30 years and the luncheon stop, however inadequate, was in those days of slow and uncomfortable travel the highlight of the journey. It was also a dire necessity, for lavatories on trains were still largely a thing of the future!

The East Coast companies selected York as the obvious stopping point. Not only does the city lie very nearly halfway between London and Edinburgh, but the station there was for many years a terminus, which meant a reversal of through trains and a change of locomotives anyway. The refreshment and dining rooms occupied the ground floor of the north wing of George Andrews' fine 1852 station buildings, the front block of which formed the first York Station Hotel (and which is now the West Offices of British Rail's Eastern Region Headquarters). Scottish expresses were allowed just twenty minutes there for refreshment, owing to competition for speed between East Coast and West Coast companies. Shorter-distance services were apt to be allocated ten minutes only. However well geared-up the staff may have been, eating proper meals was a mad scramble reminiscent of the old Wolverton experience, and the scene has been passed down to posterity in the *Illustrated London News'* famous 1872 print. When York's new, through station was opened in 1877, the arrangements were transferred to the new refreshment rooms there lock, stock and barrel.

Across on the West Coast Main line, the choice of refreshment stop also fell easily on a town at approximately the halfway point: Preston, an important junction with the platform space to accommodate long-distance trains while they waited there for up to half an hour. To make the best use of this space, the Preston refreshment rooms were built on a long central island platform – the first time such a situation was adopted. Preston, like York, was rebuilt in 1877 and the new premises featured

'Ten Minutes for refreshment.' The frantic scene as a ravenous trainload invades the refreshment rooms at York (now BR's West Offices), from the *Illustrated London News* of 7 September 1872.

another innovation – the long counter of the main bar was bent round in a U-shape, thus doubling the length of available space.

Preston refreshment rooms were to attract more than one VIP visitor before the restaurant cars did away with the need for such stops. On 21 May 1894, Queen Victoria ate there on a journey north to Balmoral after opening the Manchester Ship Canal. The manager of the railway-owned Park Hotel nearby was in charge of the catering, and roast beef was on the menu. Flowers and silver candlesticks adorned the dining room for the occasion; while the Queen dined, attended by her Indian servants, a member of the Royal Household exercised Her Majesty's two dogs along the platform outside.

Security for this occasion was tight, with the station entrance barricaded and rail traffic diverted to distant platforms. But two years later, it was even tighter for the visit of Tsar Nicholas of Russia, accompanied by the Tsarina Alexandra and their then only daughter, the little Grand Duchess Olga. Returning to

Portsmouth after visiting Queen Victoria at Balmoral, the Russian Royal family stopped for Sunday morning breakfast at Preston. Numerous assassination attempts had been made on the Tsar, and this time the station entrance was boarded up and the station barred to all traffic save the Romanoffs' special train. The dining room was a mass of floral beauty, a crimson carpet covered much of the platform, and further floral decorations hid the rest of the deserted station. Above on the roof, and in the subways below, police and guards kept an eagle eye for would-be bombers and assassins. After breakfast the Tsar and Tsarina stretched their legs along the platform. All went well, the special train departed exactly on time, and with a great sigh of relief, Preston station and its refreshment rooms began to return to normal.

The great and the good were also visitors to a less likely railway locality than York or Preston. In 1876 the Midland Railway opened its famed Settle-Carlisle main line, and with its ally the Glasgow & South Western began a new rival express service between London and Scotland. The Midland brought to this venture its reputation for superior refreshments and passenger care, and discussion as to where best to establish its luncheon stop occupied much management time. Once again a roughly halfway position was sought, with enough platform space to hold long trains for up to half an hour without getting in the way of other traffic. The choice thus fell upon Normanton, a village in the coalfields ten miles south of Leeds. Originally an obscure spot (with all due respect to its good burghers), it had grown to be a very important railway centre at the junction of the Midland, North Eastern, and Lancashire & Yorkshire systems. For the start of the new Scottish expresses, its refreshment facilities were much expanded; the telegraph office was converted into a first class dining room, though third class travellers had to make do with the rather less substantial protection of a lean-to awning and screen. On the inaugural day, 1 May 1876, the press and VIP party on the first train was treated to a banquet; the menu had been on display before departure at St Pancras, orders were collected at Leicester and telegraphed through to Normanton, so that upon arrival the first course was already on the table. Behind this event, which earned much favourable comment, lay the organisation of our old friends, Spiers and Pond.

Anglo-Scottish services at first stopped at Normanton for half an hour, but in 1888 this was whittled down to 25 minutes and in the 1890s to twenty. Six-course meals were advertised, so portions must have been on the modest side! The refreshment rooms themselves had by this time been rebuilt, along with the rest of the station, and Acworth, in his famous documentary book the *Railways of England* (1890) pays a handsome tribute by declaring: 'Even the famous buffet at Avignon would hardly furnish a dinner of six courses and coffee for half a crown, as is done for Scotch passengers at Normanton.' So for nearly three decades the name of this humble settlement was as well-known to travellers in Britain as Crewe. But while Crewe still thrives, Normanton, shorn of its connecting services and with most of its buildings razed, has sunk back into obscurity, its station but a shadow of its former self. Perhaps, on dark nights, today's belated traveller may still sense the ghosts of the scene described by Pendleton in *Our Railways*:

> 'Mingled with the rush of the express and the ringing of bells and the noise of shunting and the cries of porters, the calm, polite guard comes to the carriage door and quietly intimates that there is a ten minutes' wait if you would like a bowl of soup, ready on the marble-topped counter of the daintily-appointed refreshment room, that you can see all brilliant with light just across the platform.'

The larger refreshment rooms employed a considerable number of female staff, as we saw at Wolverton in Chapter 1, and similar arrangements had to be made for live-in accommodation for them, especially where very early and late working were part of life. The girls' living quarters came to be an accepted need. Sometimes these might be above the station buildings (where some, indeed, still remain); sometimes, as at many of the London termini, they would occupy staff quarters at the neighbouring railway hotels. At some places, this arrangement lasted until comparatively recent times, because of problems in finding suitable lodgings in the run-down neighbourhoods that surround some urban railway stations. There was much the same need at remotely-situated junctions in the country, but fewer of these have survived the cuts of the mid-twentieth century, and the rise of part-time working by older married women has reduced the problem.

Most railway companies endeavoured to keep strict control on the quality and morals of their refreshment room staff. On the London & North Western, for example, the policy for many years was to employ only the daughters of company servants. As a press report of 1906 remarked, 'This is an admirable rule. They are allowed a considerable amount of liberty, but they must obey the rule that tells them no late hours are permitted.'

In contrast to this policy of keeping things in the family, some companies preferred to keep their refreshment rooms with all their attendant problems out to contract in the hands of professional caterers. This tradition was strongest on those companies south of the Thames which, as we have seen, operated a similar policy with their on-train catering. The London, Brighton & South Coast Railway contract went to Bertrams, except for the refreshment rooms on the Brighton side of London's Victoria station, which along with the Grosvenor Hotel adjacent were operated by Gordon Hotels. The Bertrams contracts were destined to run until 1951.

On the London & South Western Railway the contract was held by Spiers & Pond, as it was on the South Eastern from 1899, and on the London, Chatham & Dover until 1905. In that year the LC&D changed to J. Lyons & Co, and this change provoked an enthusiastic, if somewhat partisan paragraph in *The Daily Telegraph*. 'Joe' Lyons obviously decided to start operations with a bang, for there was 'an average reduction in price of at least 25%,' while the quality of articles was said to have 'very materially increased, with the accommodation also largely added to.' Popular prices were the feature of all the forty restaurants on the line, while 'the reduction of the price of a cup of tea to twopence has caused the consumption of that beverage at the railway stations to be twenty times as great as formerly.' The reporter adds: 'This is not merely to be accounted for by the wave of temperance!' And as a finale: 'The Directors (of the LC&DR) can pride themselves on the fact that they were the first of any similar body to seriously consider the reform of refreshment catering. No better instance could be given of the wisdom of providing exactly what a passenger requires than the enormously increased turnover of the refreshment department since it has been under the intelligent management of J. Lyons & Co.' Nevertheless, no other railway made a similar appointment, and at the grouping of 1923 the Dover line reverted to Spiers & Pond.

SOUTH EASTERN AND CHATHAM RAILWAY.

(London, Chatham, and Dover Section.)

TO TRAVELLERS TO VICTORIA STATION.

Passengers are informed that the temporary Dining Rooms are situate on the Main Line Departure Platform and are under the management of

J. LYONS & Co. Ltd.
the well-known Caterers.

Entrees, Joints, Grill, etc. from 1/-

Cold Meats - - from 10d.

Beverages at Popular Prices.

HIGH-CLASS CUISINE. . . . . . .

FRENCH & GERMAN SPOKEN.

Also at Ludgate Hill Station.

SOUTH EASTERN AND CHATHAM RAILWAY

(London, Chatham, and Dover Section).

ABRIDGED TARIFF OF
BUFFET & TEA ROOMS
. . AT . .
VICTORIA, ST. PAUL'S, AND LUDGATE HILL STATIONS.

And at Margate (West). Ramsgate Harbour. Dover Harbour, Canterbury (East), Herne Bay, Faversham. etc. etc.

Caterers : J. LYONS & Co Ltd.

Tea (freshly made for each person)	per cup	2d
Coffee	per cup	2d
Cocoa	per cup	2d
Milk	per glass	1d
Mineral Waters		1½d & 3d
Scotch Whisky		3d & 4d
Stout (Reid's)	per glass	2d
Algerian Claret		1 3
Graves		2 6
Beaune		3 -
Hennessy's Brandy		6d & 1/-
Cold Roast Beef		6d
Ham		6d
Pork Pie		3d
Baton (specially) or Bread		1d
Buttered Toast		2d

Confectionery, Tobacco, Cigarettes, and Cigars also at Popular Prices.

OVER.

J. Lyons & Co's tariff for London, Chatham & Dover Railway stations from 1905. *J. Lyons & Co.*

In 1930 the Southern Railway, as it was by then, put all its Spiers & Pond contracts out to open tender, and the winner this time was Frederick Hotels, already giving good service on the Southern cross-channel steamers. Frederick's continued to hold these contracts right up to Nationalisation in 1948.

Both Frederick's and Gordon's owed their existence to Frederick Gordon himself, the eminent hotelier who personally retained the chairmanship of Frederick's. A chairman of Gordon Hotels was to be F. W. Towle, son of William Towle, Director of Hotels and Catering on the Midland Railway. The finance for Gordon's venture had come from Sir John Blundell Maple, MP, head of the great furnishing empire, who as we shall see in a later chapter, also financed the hotels for the Great Central Railway. A business associate of Maple's was Lord Dalziel of Wooler, head of Pullman in Britain from 1907 to 1927, which had the train catering contracts for the southern companies other than the South Western. So between them, a small group of business moguls had the railway catering business in the southern counties well sewn up! The absorption of Frederick's by the Hotels Executive of the British Transport Commission, after Nationalisation in 1948, was thus little more than formalising control of an already closely-integrated concern.

Contracting-out of refreshment rooms was also the rule on the Midland Railway until 1877, when for the first time William Towle began to bring them directly under railway management. Spiers & Pond, as we have seen, had a nationwide portfolio of leases. On the Great Western, the firm of Browning & Wesley in 1895 operated 23 refreshment rooms between Paddington and Birkenhead and in the West Midlands, while numerous small contractors operated along the main line to Bristol, with the GWR itself directly managing only 11, all in the West Country. Leasing was also the rule for the numbers of railway-owned inns bought or built in the heady days of the mid-nineteenth century Railway Mania. Some such pubs, like the Wellington opposite Waterloo, were close by railway stations (and indeed the Wellington recently reverted for a short while to direct railway management, under the Travellers-Fare banner). Others were rather more remote, and none more so than the Pilot Inn, on the marshes near Dungeness in Kent, part of the construction of which was once formed by the upturned hull of an old ship.

From the turn of the century, direct management by the railways (Southern companies apart) increasingly began to find favour, and this trend accelerated after the retirement in 1904 of Felix Spiers (Christopher Pond having died some years earlier). William Towle on the Midland Railway had formed a headquarters department to run all the company's hotels, refreshment rooms and restaurant cars as early as 1871, and this centralised form of control was also adopted on the Midland's great rival, the London & North Western. The Great Western started rather later, but it too formed a hotels and catering headquarters at Paddington, and by the 1920s was able to announce proudly in its publicity brochures that its refreshment rooms all came 'under the direct Management of the Company.'

A slightly different direction was taken by the companies on the East side of Britain – the companies destined to be merged to form the London & North Eastern Railway at the Grouping in 1923. Here, catering managers tended to report not to a catering *eminence grise* at company headquarters, but to local general management. There was thus less of a centralised policy concerning the refreshment rooms, and little in the way of what today we would call a corporate image. There were those who

Despite its humble wooden structure Colchester down side refreshment room, pictured here about 1900, was made the subject of this sepia Victorian postcard. The Great Eastern Railway timetable hangs inside the door. *Author's collection.*

claimed the rooms were better and friendlier places for it!

Business at the refreshment rooms was affected, as ever, by the locations they occupied, and this in turn affected their style. A popular development, for those rooms able to tap a good lunchtime trade from a business neighbourhood, was the Grill Room and its close relative, the Business Luncheon Room. These rooms had much of the comfort of a traditional dining room, but offered a less formal and time-consuming menu and had a style of their own. A number of them became well-established and fashionable meeting places, and one such, the Lancashire & Yorkshire Railway's Grill Room at Manchester Victoria, opened 1905, occupied a very handsomely-appointed Edwardian room featuring a fine stained-glass dome. It is very pleasing to note that though the trade in this part of Manchester has changed a great deal, the building, maintained in much of its original style, is still a popular refreshment spot today. Up in the Capital, *Pitman's Journal* of 21 March 1908 saw fit to remark:

> 'We wonder how many of our readers know that, right in the City, there is an excellent station restaurant where one of the best dinners obtainable in London is served daily by the London & North-Western Railway. We refer to the restaurant in Broad Street Station, where the catering is done by the Company itself, the waiters wearing the neat uniform of railway attendants'.

The building of luncheon rooms also had an eye to other rather less expected clienteles, as an article in the *Birmingham Daily Mail* of 24 September 1915 reminds us. Reporting on the opening of the new luncheon room at Nuneaton, the *Mail* observed: 'It is intended to popularise the new establishment as a high-class tea room for ladies, for whom the lack of provision of this kind had been greatly felt at all times, but especially during the hunting season'. Such a link between the very different worlds of hunting and station catering may strike today's readers as a shade incongruous, but in those days the horsey set, like everyone else, still depended on the railway for all except the shortest of journeys.

By the 1920s, luncheon rooms or dining rooms with waitress service were gracing most stations with any pretensions to importance as well as some where trade must have been highly seasonal, such as Ballater, Scarborough, or Newton Abbot. The London Midland & Scottish Railway, formed at the Grouping of

RILL ROOM & RESTAURANT,
IA STATION, MANCHESTER.

Telephone: 6178
Telegrams: "Stimulant"

The Lancashire & Yorkshire Railway's Grill Room and Restaurant at Manchester Victoria, opened 1905. (Note the telegraphic address, 'Stimulant'!) Compare the same view 80 years on, page 197. *Author's collection.*

1923, used to issue platform tickets endorsed 'Free of charge between 12 noon and 3.0pm to enable the holder to take luncheon in the dining room'. This recognised the problem of rooms located on island platforms, where they would lack a street entrance – handy for rail travellers but hardly an incentive to High Street trade.

A few large termini boasted a full-blown restaurant, such as the well-known Great Western one at Birmingham Snow Hill, made much of in the company's publicity. This luxurious rendezvous, offering a full service of *à-la-carte* and *table d'hôte* meals on the grand scale, occupied much of the ground floor of the former Great Western Hotel. This hotel had been a privately-owned venture designed to capitalise on trade from the station, at the same time providing luxury accommodation for the Birmingham smart set. For one reason or another – and surprisingly, in view of the success of railway-owned station hotels elsewhere – the venture failed. As early as 1906 the building was bought by the GWR, the ground floor became the restaurant, and the upper floors were converted to offices for railway staff.

Such then was the range of refreshment rooms which had grown out of the original ideas, and with which the railway companies of Britain beguiled their customers in their heyday. A few added extra touches, more expected of a hotel than a refreshment room; copies of *The Times* newspaper, for example, were available for reading in Edwardian days in the Midland Railway's rooms at Sheffield, Nottingham, and Leicester. In Scotland, the Caledonian Railway was noted for its Wedgwood design china, its fine drapery and cream-and-gold tablecloths. While in the Highlands, we might mention another and different example of a place that achieved a nationwide reputation entirely by virtue of its refreshment room. The little village of Crianlarich stands where the former North British line from Glasgow to Fort William crosses over the Caledonian line from Callander to Oban. There is a junction, and more importantly a crossing loop on the Fort William line, where ever since its opening trains have been subject to lengthy stops awaiting traffic coming in the opposite direction. Crianlarich station is also a favourite jumping-off point for hikers and climbers. The fortifying refreshments served to these various customers, and the romantic setting of the place, turned it into something of a legend; although the place has lost much of its style and has been in private hands for many years, something of the tradition still lives on today.

Unfortunately, by no means all refreshment rooms had the attractions of some of those described above, and the old 'Mugby Junction' image tended to linger on in the public mind. Behind this lay a number of trends, not the fault of the rooms themselves, the significance of which was not properly grasped by the management of the time. One of course was the coming of the restaurant cars, with all their public appeal and their complexities, and the amount of time they took up among railway catering management. Another concerned the changing layout of stations. As the technicalities of railways grew more sophisticated, companies everywhere discovered that the station premises of the early years were nowhere near adequate to cope with new operating demands; the generous provision of multiple refreshment facilities, which hogged so much valuable building space, began to be cut down. Further, as stations were added to, their centre of gravity tended to move away from the original building containing the catering, leaving the facilities inconveniently sited. A good example of this was at Bletchley, where the main refreshment room on the ground floor of the Station Hotel, was left high and dry by the extension of the station eastwards in a series of island platforms, which took the main traffic flows with it. A small additional room was eventually provided, and the original one closed.

The public, as consumers, were more concerned with matters like prices. Railway caterers traditionally offer a service for extended hours and at weekends, creating staff costs well above those in the High Street, and this of course is reflected in the price of food and drink. Today these problems are shared on the motorways and at the airports, but up until the 1950s railway prices were in a league of their own and to the passenger, heedless of the reasons, this stood out like a sore thumb. For many years the average price of a cup of railway tea was 4d (2p), compared to 2d (1p) or 2½d elsewhere. An angry writer to the *Daily Chronicle* in 1903 observed that he had been in correspondence with the manager of the refreshment rooms of the London & North Western Railway, but without result. 'I notice' he continued, 'that in some parts of England the companies have been compelled to reduce their extortionate charge for tea, in consequence of objection being taken to the renewal of the licenses before the Licensing Justices. I intend to adopt this course in one or two places next year at the Licensing Sessions.' This sounds perilously close to blackmail, and it reminds us that Licencees could (and can) be at risk from controversial matters other than just alcohol.

The London & North Western Railway came under fire from its own staff over its tea prices, which were viewed by those who did not have the responsibility of balancing the books as actively driving business away. A letter in the *Railway Review* for 11 March 1910 makes a plea not only for cheaper beverages, but for refreshment rooms to be kept open throughout the night (which would no doubt have yielded juicy staff overtime). 'We have long contended,' says the writer, 'that the railway companies possessed a veritable gold mine if they did but run their refreshment rooms on business lines.' He quite forgot to mention the widespread custom of the railways selling certain popular lines to their staff at ½d or 1d less than public prices; such items, according to a GWR tariff dated 1909, included not only tea and coffee but also plated meals, meat pasties, and draught beer.

Behind the scenes: the Swindon refreshment room kitchens in 1901. The primitive and unhygienic look of this place would hardly have helped the railways in their battle against music-hall jokes and public complaints. *GWR Museum, Swindon.*

Then there were the quality of the food and the attitude of the staff. 'There is the dirty counter first of all,' says a contributor to *Ideas* magazine in April 1905,

'and there are the haughty duchesses (in disguise) behind it. I have in my mind's eye a lady of mature years who presides over the destinies of a buffet in the south of this island. Her rule is iron. Her satellites tremble at her nod. The returns are from Liquor, not food; when anybody . . . proceeds to demand refreshment of a solid nature, this lady literally glares at him. "Don't make them too comfortable, girls!" is the motto here.

'Then, as to the solids supplied, there is the fossilised bun, a special creation of the Noah's Ark period, when its keeping properties must have been of very direct service during the duration of the deluge. Then we come to the sandwiches. Often described as "ham", I have found them to consist of a species of muscular tissue which may have been that of the horse, or even dog or cat.

'The only persons who enjoy these things, washing them down with a liquid called "coffee" (but which resembles ditch water in appearance, and does not possess the refreshing taste of that fluid) are curates of tender age, whose digestive organs, from a long course of ascetic feeding, can suffer and be strong under anything which fills a vacuum.'

Whether the curates of the land took offence at this unwarranted provocation is not recorded, and neither is the railways' response to the suggestion that dreadful food and frosty service were a deliberate part of a scheme to bundle out the eaters as quickly as possible and concentrate on the more profitable boozers. What is recorded, however, is a riposte by that high priest of catering on the Midland Railway, William Towle. Well aware of the efforts being made to improve the refreshment scene, and obviously sick to death of such complaints rumbling on, Towle in 1914 wrote in the *Railway News*:

'I think it quite unnecessary to repeat, much less to refute, the strange medley of ancient jibes, humourous and sarcastic, levelled against the old refreshment rooms. I have, in the interests of the public and in a fairly critical mood, compared . . . an average English refreshment room, say, at Leicester Midland Station, with one of the temperance cafes or tea rooms run by most popular caterers in London, and I find that . . . in every respect the railway refreshment room is superior.

'It is open to any of your readers or railway critics to test this. I am forced to the conclusion that the unfair criticism of railway management which one is always hearing is part of a newspaper campaign generally against railways, which is ungenerous, unfair, and against which in other matters besides catering it is time a protest was made.'

So there! It is very unlikely that the newspapers were consciously campaigning against railways as a whole, though in the heyday of private railway companies, some indeed came in for more criticism than others. But the popular papers, with their penchant for bad news, were like dogs reluctant to let an old bone go, particularly one which for 50 years had faithfully filled blank columns when no meatier 'news' was around.

The outbreak of World War I in 1914 largely put a stop to major railway work until after the Grouping in 1923, which formed the four great railway companies – London Midland & Scottish; London & North Eastern; Great Western; and Southern. The catering on the last-named continued to be let out to contractors, but for all concerned the period after the war was a difficult one. With road transport in the ascendant, the level of passenger traffic was beginning to feel the effects, and there were problems, too, with some of the railway hotels which were

Birmingham Snow Hill (GWR) refreshment rooms in 1926: part of a story of declining profits. Note the displays of snack boxes for taking onto trains. *Travellers Fare*.

still rooted in an age that, as people were coming to realise, had gone for ever. Hotels and dining cars had long been a more rewarding and glamorous world to manage than humdrum station catering, so now, more than ever, that was where the railways directed their resources.

There was little progress in the development of refreshment rooms, and this in turn encouraged trade to fall away faster, leading to closures and further cutbacks – a classic vicious spiral. The GWR refreshment rooms, for example, produced a peak profit of nearly £80,000 in 1918; thereafter, though the takings held more or less steady, profits steadily fell away to a meagre £13,000 by 1932, when the Depression was really biting. A re-think of the whole scene was long overdue. What actually happened we shall discover in a later chapter.

4
Grand Hotel

As the steam engine began to turn railways into a practical means of long-distance travel, it became clear that passengers would need not only refreshment, but also a night's rest upon their journey. For though a tremendous advance on anything that had gone before, railway travel was still comparatively slow and uncertain. A basic network of lines not yet complete, lengthy detours, or gaps filled by stagecoach or even coastal ship, meant the hardy traveller had to spend a night or more upon his journey.

The stagecoach inns, besides being in the wrong places, were as inadequate for accommodating railway travellers as they were for refreshing them, so local entrepreneurs began to seize upon the chance of rich pickings by putting up new hotels close by railway stations. Soon the railway companies themselves realised the possibilities, and in 1838 the London & Birmingham Railway, even before it was fully open, issued its shareholders a prospectus for a new venture called the London & Birmingham Railway & Dormitories. This was a subsidiary company set up to build the hotel, for in those days there was a law designed to protect investors, that forbade railway companies to spend shareholders' money on anything except railways themselves.

Work soon started at Euston to a design by Philip Hardwick, architect of the famous Doric Arch; on one side of the station approach stood a third class dormitory block and breakfast room, named the Victoria after the new monarch, while across the way the Euston Hotel offered superior accommodation for first class travellers. In September 1839, the Victoria became the very first railway-owned hotel to open its doors for business, while the Euston opposite followed three months later.

The management of these two hotels took a little time to arrange. At first, the Victoria was let to one Robert Bacon, former steward of the Athenaeum Club, while after some haggling the Euston went to Messrs J. Dethier and Z. Vantini, who also ran the company's refreshment rooms at Wolverton. Late in 1840 Robert Bacon moved north to the L&B's new hotel in Birmingham, at that time also called the Victoria (but later 'Hardwick's Queen'), while Dethier and Vantini took over both Euston establishments, running them as one; it was to be another forty-odd years before these two buildings became structurally joined.

Meanwhile in 1844 Monsieur Dethier, who hailed from Brussels, split with his partner and set up on his own, taking on other leases, including the Great Northern Hotel at King's Cross when that opened ten years later. This left Vantini in sole charge at Euston. Zenon Vantini, a Corsican by birth, was a character as colourful as his name and was said to have been a courier to Napoleon before reaching British shores. Volatile and enthusiastic by temperament, he now cast around for new outlets for his energy and soon found himself involved in another grand piece of Victorian speculation.

One of the biggest constraints on the building of large hotels before the Companies Act of 1862 was the law severely restricting the number of shareholders in any organisation. This in turn limited the amount of capital available, but railway companies were exempt from these restraints and could thus raise the capital for really large hotels. Otherwise, an individual needed to be very rich before joining this particular fray. Just such a person was Sir Peter Hesketh Fleetwood, MP, of Rossall Hall on the Lancashire coast. Fleetwood's dream was to create a major new port, rivalling Liverpool, on the flatlands of the River Wyre estuary, and he now invested a considerable part of his fortune in building the new Fleetwood Docks, as well as the Preston & Wyre Railway, the town of Fleetwood itself, and a fine hotel which opened in 1841 and which he named the North Euston. This hotel had all the style of a great railway establishment, and the manager appointed to run it was Zenon Vantini. The hotel's name was no idle fantasy, for the ferry services already operating from Fleetwood were joined in 1844 by a regular steamer to Ardrossan on the Ayrshire coast, whence trains connected to Glasgow. With completion of the West Coast railway route to Scotland still four years away, the North Euston became an important staging post on the London–Glasgow journey. But there were navigational difficulties when entering the new Fleetwood harbour, and when the southbound boat finally docked, passengers were apt to find that the London train had left. This meant 24 hours' delay and an expensive night in the hotel, whereupon the name must have struck the traveller, stranded two hundred miles north of his real destination, as somewhat ironic!

Inns and hotels, often called 'The Station', 'The Railway' or by the name of the local railway company, now sprang up next to stations in many places, and a number of them are there to this day. Most of the smaller ones were private ventures, though some were built by the railway themselves. That at Swindon, combined with refreshment rooms, has already been described in Chapter 1, but the hotel has long since been converted to offices. The Crewe Arms Hotel, built privately in 1837, ministers to travellers still. Leased by the London & North Western Railway in 1864 and subsequently bought outright, it was heavily rebuilt in 1880, but a railway-associated hotel has nevertheless stood longer on this site than anywhere else, probably in the world. At Derby, the splendid Cuff's Station Hotel, opened in 1841, had stronger railway links from the start, as it was specifically designed by Francis Thompson to match his railway station across the road; in 1862 it was bought by the railway and re-named the Midland, and this historic building survives today, unlike Crewe, in much its original state.

Euston was sadly demolished in 1963 and is thus out of the reckoning. Apart from Birmingham Curzon Street (1840) and Swindon (1841), railways built small hotels at Colchester (1843) and Gateshead (1844); but like many speculative ventures of those days they were not a success and were soon closed or sold. But in 1847 the Furness Railway, keen to spread its empire, purchased a seventeenth-century manor house near Barrow-in-Furness which it extended and opened as the Furness Abbey Hotel. This was partly to serve the rapidly-expanding industrial area round Barrow, but the company also had an eye to tourist business visiting the nearby Lake District. Even so, to advertise it (as the railway did) as being 'in the heart of English Lakeland' was stretching the facts somewhat, and would certainly have fallen foul of today's Trades Descriptions Act.

The following year, 1848, saw two more railway hotels built – both on the coast. The North Western at Morecambe (later re-named the Midland) looked first and foremost to the holiday trade; in the 1930s it was knocked down and a completely new

Lost Leviathan: this lithograph shows the LBSCR's London & Paris Hotel, Newhaven, at its opening in 1848. This once-famous Channel landmark was damaged in a 1942 air raid and later demolished. *Newhaven Historical Society collection.*

hotel built on the site, which remains a well-known rendezvous to this day. The London, Brighton & South Coast Railway's London & Paris Hotel at Newhaven, however, was self-evidently there for the ferry trade. This hotel was leased out throughout its working life, the first lessee being one Bacon – very possibly the same Bacon who eight years earlier had launched the Euston hotel on its way, for men with experience of catering on such a scale were few and far between in those days. The London & Paris suffered bomb damage while under Admiralty requisition in 1942 and was never reopened, being demolished in 1958.

In 1849 the North Staffordshire Railway completed the fine North Stafford Hotel at Stoke-on-Trent, and this is now the earliest large-scale railway-built (as against railway-bought) hotel still going in much its original form. This fine building, something of an architectural showpiece, was leased out from the start – initially to Mr Cuff, of the Station (later Midland) Hotel at Derby. The leasing continued for all save the last 21 years (1932–1953) of its railway ownership. Such leasing-out and leasing-in was common with many of the older hotels, and the history of this is both confusing and patchily documented.

A rush of hotel building now followed, and two establishments completed in 1851, the Great Northern at Peterborough and the Royal Station at Hull, were fully railway-managed right up to their sale in 1983, thus each achieving a record 132 years in railway service.

The building of hotels in what were then rather unlikely 'green-field' areas was a ploy now indulged by a number of railway builders and railway companies. The real name of this game was to make as much money as possible. 'Green-field' land was still very cheap, as was land in run-down urban districts, where the railway also bought heavily. The idea was that by building a station and a hotel, a community would develop, requiring all kinds of other buildings, pushing up the price of land and making the promoters rich men. Sometimes railways themselves undertook (though subsidiary companies) whole town developments, with the hotel forming the focal point of the community, rather like Sir Peter Hesketh Fleetwood's ventures. A particularly good example grew up at Saltburn on the North Yorkshire Coast, where the town and the Zetland Hotel were planned by what had been the world's first public steam railway, the Stockton & Darlington, though the company was taken over by the North Eastern while the hotel (opened in 1863) was being built.

In Britain's city centres no land was particularly cheap, and there was intense competition between railway companies and private hoteliers for the best sites. Proximity was all; in Birmingham, the LNWR had its own Queens Hotel right over the station, whereupon the private Midland Hotel, across the way, had the cheek to take upon itself the telegraphic address 'Nearest, Birmingham'. Conversely, lack of competition tended to subdue the hotel-building programme. The Great Western Railway, with its near monopoly of large areas of the West, opened its splendid Great Western Hotel at Paddington in 1854, just missing the 1851 Great Exhibition, which had prompted the idea, but thereafter had added only three by the turn of the century (and two of those were acquired with the takeover of the South Wales Railway). The GWR in all truth may well have been warned off by experience with the original refreshment room contract at Swindon, with its constantly changing tenants and its association with bad coffee and that dreaded compulsory

William Towle (1849–1929), hotel and catering manager of the Midland Railway, and 'grandfather' of the British railway hotel business. *Caterer & Hotelkeeper.*

ten-minute stop. At all events the policy persisted, and the cities of the West such as Bristol, Plymouth and Cardiff never did possess their railway-owned hotels.

But it was the Midland Railway, with its prime tradition of passenger comfort, which led the way in the hotels saga. In 1864, soon after buying the station hotel in Derby, the Midland had taken into its employ there one William Towle, a fifteen-year-old village lad from Twyford, just south of the town. Humble origins proved no obstacle to quick progress, and the reputation of Towle as a young Turk, as one might put it, soon reached the ears of senior management. By 1871 he was Manager of the hotel; four years later he began his famous lunch basket service for railway passengers, described in a later chapter, and by 1892 he was General Manager of all the Midland's hotels, dining cars and refreshment rooms. He was to retire as Sir William in 1914, whereupon his sons Arthur and Francis became joint controllers of the business. Francis later left to become Chairman of Gordon Hotels, while Arthur until his retirement in 1944 served as Controller of the LMS Hotel Services, using the telegraphic address 'Towlamid, London.'

William Towle's brief as Hotels chief was very simply to make the Midland's hotels supreme, attracting traffic from rival lines and bringing in local function business to top-up the railway's coffers. To add to the Midland at Derby, Towle now had the company's massive London flagship – the Midland Grand at St Pancras, first opened in 1873, though not fully completed for another three years.

This awe-inspiring monument to Victorian Gothic architecture was the brainchild of George Gilbert Scott who, entering a competition for the hotel's design, calmly re-wrote the specification to suit himself, adding two extra floors to the plans and an extra £50,000 to the proposed £350,000 cost. Scott must have had great confidence in his own fashionability, for despite the understandable protests of the other ten contestants, he won. Midland Chairman James Allport had been determined to bring his provincial company up to Town with the maximum of grandeur, and surely did he succeed, for ever since its opening day the building has towered over a wide neighbourhood, for all the world like the Midland Railway's terminus in the Eternal City.

Four hundred bedrooms, and a dining room 100ft long, 30ft wide and 24ft high were the basic amenities of this enormous pile. Upper floor bedrooms, smaller than those below, were the domain of the servants of the gentlefolk who occupied more spacious apartments beneath. To reach the upper storeys, the hotel installed the new-fangled device of 'rising rooms', or hydraulic lifts, complete with shaded, Heath Robinson-like diagrams intended to put guests' minds at ease about the safety of those contraptions – but which may well have done the reverse. There is in fact no record of any of these 'rising rooms' having made a sudden and disastrous descent, but in 1883 a Mr Smith somehow wandered into a service area near his bedroom in the middle of the night and fell straight down a lift shaft to his death. The shaft must have been inadequately guarded to say the least, yet the Midland Railway won its appeal against the £3,500 damages awarded to the family of the deceased.

Advertisement for Midland Railway hotels in the 1890 *Post Office London Guide*. The 'flagship' is the Midland Grand, St Pancras; the Adelphi in Liverpool was not yet purchased, nor the Midland in Manchester built. *Westminster City Libraries*.

Running water in bedrooms was unknown in those days, and for morning ablutions there was a washstand in each bedroom and a tin bath under the bed. Guests rang the bell to summon the chambermaid, whose ewer of hot water, carried from the distant back regions, was often tepid by the time it arrived. The corridors to be negotiated were vast – always wide enough to let two ladies in crinolines pass each other – and heating everywhere was by means of coal fires in each room, with the coal having to be carted round the building in scuttles and buckets. Upon the roof stood a veritable forest of chimneys, each one numbered to correspond with the room it served so that if, for example, the occupant of No 174 reported foul fumes blowing back, the offending bird's nest could be quickly tracked down and removed.

With the Midland Grand firmly established in the capital, William Towle set out to extend his empire to the other big cities on the Midland's territory, buying existing hotels in Leeds and Liverpool and building a new one in Bradford. But the biggest need was in the city of Manchester, and Towle planned a particularly fine edifice in the new Midland Hotel there, which opened in 1903. This hotel, to the design of the eminent Charles Trubshaw, was in a totally different league from anything else in or around Manchester. As well as its luxurious suites, French restaurant and Turkish baths, it boasted its own sub-post office and an 800-seat theatre, which lasted until 1922. Such was the impact of the new hotel that the chairman of hoteliers Spiers & Pond, moving the adoption of the company's 1905/6 annual report, commented that

'some of the increased competition . . . was not fair, as in the case of the Midland Railway Hotel at Manchester, which had cost the railway company, he was told, £1¼ million . . . Every other hotel in Manchester was practically doing no business, for the new hotel was more than sufficient to supply all the wants of Manchester. It was not the original intention that the railways should launch out into that sort of business.'

It seems more than likely that Spiers & Pond was particularly peeved through having recently lost Midland refreshment room contracts to Towle's in-house control!

These massive hotels were looked upon, like restaurant cars, as an essential back-up service to the company's main business and their actual profitability was becoming a rather sensitive

Liverpool's vast North Western Hotel (later the Lime Street), opened 1871 and seen here in its early years, was later overshadowed by the more fashionable Adelphi. It closed in 1933 and has remained a 'white elephant' ever since. *Crown Copyright. National Railway Museum, York.*

issue, with shareholders' questions on the matter apt to be circumnavigated. But undaunted, Towle had also embarked on the enlargement of the Queens in Leeds in 1898, and then the complete rebuilding of the Adelphi in Liverpool, completed in 1914. If possible, this was even more imposing than its Manchester sister, looming above the city centre like the ocean liners to whose passengers it ministered. Indeed, the whole style and decor deliberately had the feel of grand maritime architecture, with staterooms and cabin-style bedroom doors opening outwards rather than inwards. The Adelphi claimed for decades to be the social centre of Merseyside, putting the huge but old-fashioned LNWR hotel at Lime Street (1871) in the shade – and so indeed it was, no more so than on Grand National nights, when some of the stories of horses being ridden up the grand staircase might not have been all that far-fetched.

The Midland's empire under the Towle 'dynasty' represented the grandest and finest of the railway hotel chains. Its traditions lasted (for good or ill) right until the break-up of British Transport Hotels in the 1980s. Meanwhile, other developments were afoot elsewhere, such as at the ferry ports which early became a natural focus for hotel building.

The grandest, and for a long time the busiest of these was the South Eastern Railway's Lord Warden Hotel at Dover, opened in 1853 and named after the then venerable Duke of Wellington, Lord Warden of the Cinque Ports. The South Eastern directors pursued the same policy with their hotels as they did with their railway catering and sought a professional hotelier to manage it, on a tenancy basis; in 1896 it was sold on long lease to Gordon Hotels. By this time it had become a base for the catering services on the railway cross-channel steamers, similar arrangements being struck at the Pavilion, Folkestone, the London & Paris, Newhaven, and the South Western, Southampton.

An oddity in the south-east corner of Britain was the diminutive Port Victoria Hotel, operated by the South Eastern on the Medway estuary. This nine-bedroom wooden structure opened in 1882 as part of an ambitious scheme by the South Eastern's Chairman, Sir Edward Watkin, for a continental ferry service rivalling the established channel ports. Watkin's dream never became reality, but for many years a ferry service operated to Queenborough on the opposite side of the Medway;

more important, Port Victoria pier was not infrequently used by the Royal Yachts of both Great Britain and Germany. But Port Victoria's greatest years were from 1900 to 1904 when the mail ferry service to Flushing in Holland was transferred from Queenborough when the pier there was burned down. After that, decline was gradual but inevitable, yet in 1948 at Nationalisation this obscure outpost was re-discovered, still a going concern (just), on the list of railway hostelries operated on contract by Frederick Hotels. A visit revealed the furniture to be in such poor condition that it was deemed 'entirely unsuitable for present-day use.' Lighting was by paraffin lamp and calor gas – there was no electricity, and water was brought daily by railway locomotive. Further, because of Admiralty access restrictions, the only approach was now by boat to a jetty 200yd away! Shortly after this visit the Port Victoria Hotel was closed, the site quickly being obliterated by the new Isle of Grain petrochemical plant.

Back in less obscure waters, railway hotels were also needed for the Irish Sea services, and the London & North Western built three: at Holyhead, Dublin (North Wall) and Greenore in what is now the Irish Republic. Greenore, with its golf course and holiday bungalows, was planned as a major Irish leisure resort, but in this it never gained the status of Portrush on the Antrim coast. Here the Midland Railway acquired the elegant Northern Counties Hotel when it took over the Belfast & Northern

The Fishguard Bay Hotel, photographed here about 1920, never quite fulfilled the Great Western Railway's hopes. *BR/OPC*.

Counties Railway in 1903; along with this railway there also came the Station Hotel in Belfast, and together with the later addition of the Laharna in Larne these completed a quintet of Irish hotels owned by English railways.

Further south, the Great Western had in 1898 acquired a hotel called the Wyncliff near Fishguard as part of a deal with the Fishguard and Rosslare Railways & Harbours Company. The GWR was keen to develop trade for transatlantic liners calling at Fishguard, introducing through dining car expresses from London, so the hotel was modernised and enlarged to suit. The name Wyncliff, with its overtones of aspidistras and tea at six, was dropped and the altogether grander Fishguard Bay Hotel substituted, the establishment reopening in 1906. World War I put paid to the Fishguard transatlantic trade, and the town and its hotel had to adjust to the less glamorous but still worthwhile role of jumping-off point for Southern Ireland. But it may be significant that right up to its sale by the railways in 1950, the Fishguard Bay Hotel never once showed a profit.

Another style of railway hotel was the leisure resort fed by the company's services. Apart from the Furness Abbey already mentioned, the GWR in 1878 bought Tregenna Castle, an eighteenth-century country mansion near St Ives in Cornwall, fitting it as a luxury retreat for well-to-do customers. No sooner had it opened than a well-to-do dog disgraced itself on an expensive new carpet, and canine guests were henceforth banned from the premises! There followed other holiday ventures, such as the Lochalsh (formerly an inn, Lochalsh House) purchased by the Highland Railway at Kyle of Lochalsh, while in 1899 the impecunious Great North of Scotland Railway built the Cruden Bay Hotel near the village Port Erroll, on the coast north of Aberdeen. There was a fine golf course, too, which opened a year before the hotel (in true Scots fashion). As the hotel was a mile from the railway station, an electric tramway was built to connect the two, using the rather odd gauge of 3ft 6¼in. This tramway carried passengers until 1932 and remained opened for a further nine years after that, ferrying to and from the hotel all the laundry from the GNSR dining cars and its Palace and Station hotels in Aberdeen. Strangely enough, a few months after the tramway closed in 1941 the Palace Hotel, much the biggest user of linen on the GNS, was badly damaged by fire with the loss of six lives, and never

CENTRAL STATION HOTEL, GLASGOW.
CALEDONIAN RAILWAY.
C. LORD
MANAGER

Glasgow's Central Hotel, opened 1883, was later the home of the Malmaison, for many years Scotland's finest restaurant. *Crown Copyright. National Railway Museum, York.*

reopened. Thereafter, laundry work at the Cruden Bay was light.

Scotland was indeed proving a profitable hunting ground for railway-promoted holidays, for in the nineteenth century the geography of the country had much restricted the growth of roads and coaching inns, and the railways were drawing on a much less cluttered board. The 'density' of hotels per head of population grew to be much higher than in England; some claimed that led to the pervasive Scots influence in British Transport Hotels which, William Towle's legacy notwithstanding, lasted right up to the end. The Glasgow & South Western Railway, another line barely in the first division of British companies, now acquired the very fine new golf course laid out at Turnberry in 1901 and built an hotel of the calibre to match it, which opened in 1906. The Highland did the same with the Dornoch Hotel and golf course in 1904, followed by Strathpeffer in 1911, while the greatest of them all, Gleneagles at Auchterarder in Perthshire, was devised by Caledonian general manager Donald Mathieson about the same time. The outbreak of World War I prevented this highland palace (for such it was) from being completed until 1924.

Gleneagles, designed from the start as Britain's No 1 hotel for what today we call the jet set, quickly succeeded beyond Donald Mathieson's wildest hopes. With the Caledonian Railway by now absorbed into the LMS, its hotels controller was William Towle's son Arthur, and the resources he poured into Gleneagles were huge. Beside its two championship golf courses laid out by the great James Braid (two more have been added since), the hotel had the first French restaurant in Scotland. So successful was this that a second was opened in 1927 at another ex-Caledonian hotel, the Central in Glasgow, where the decor and the name were taken from Chateau Malmaison, home of Napoleon's Empress Josephine. The summertime 'dog days' for business in Glasgow coincided with the height of the season in Gleneagles, so Towle established the tradition of the Glasgow chef and his kitchen brigade moving to Gleneagles for the holiday weeks of high summer. As they dined, Gleneagles guests would be serenaded by another famous name – bandleader Henry Hall, who starting at the Midland in Manchester, had quickly risen to head of entertainment for all the LMS hotels, later moving on to become dance supremo at the BBC.

The big dance orchestras of the 1920s and 1930s naturally gravitated to the railway hotels, for that was where the biggest ballrooms were. Grandest of all tended to be those of the former Midland Railway, but there were others like Jos. Q. Atkinson and his Royal Station Hotel Orchestra, for a generation of swingers the sound of sophistication in Newcastle and the North-East.

Big bands and fine food, though costly in themselves, were one of the hotels' answers to the problem of keeping business up during slack periods. At the leisure hotels, the whole of the winter time was very slack; places like Gleneagles and Dornoch closed completely from October till Easter. In the cities the problem was different, for while weekdays usually brought a steady flow of business travellers, weekends would be very quiet apart from local functions. Both these factors were often quoted by Towle and his colleagues in defence of the high charges at railway hotels, for the facilities (and often the staff) were there, whether used or not, and had to be paid for.

Only in a few cases did a hotel manage to combine business with leisure and long-stay with short-stay custom. One such place was (and still is) Edinburgh, where the rival North British and Caledonian Hotels stand at either end of Princes Street as monuments to their city's attractions. The Caledonian (opened 1903) had a reputation as the more fashionable and lively rendezvous, but the North British (1902) is the more interesting building. This railway's company offices had to be knocked down to allow the hotel to be built, for they occupied the only site not in line with the Bank of Scotland nearby – and the Bank had invoked an ancient law to restrict severely any railway buildings in the area. The new edifice became one of the most gradiloquent of all railway hotels; William Towle from the Midland advised on fittings and furnishings, while NBR Hotel Committee chairman George Wieland blended the exclusive North British Whisky in the cellars. There were smoking lounges, billiard rooms, commercial travellers' writing rooms, a palm court lounge and American bar, the whole being heated by steam boilers fuelled directly from railway wagons on a siding running into the basement. With a nice reciprocal touch, these boilers until very recently supplied Waverley Station, immediately below the hotel, with steam for carriage-heating and point cleaning.

The British railway hotel business in Edwardian days had grown to be the largest in the world and was familiar ground to Royalty, Heads of State, potentates and celebrities of every kind. Charles Rolls and Henry Royce held their first historic meeting in the Midland in Manchester. At the other end of the political spectrum, the Communist Party of Great Britain was founded in London's Cannon Street Hotel in 1920! The hotels owned their own laundries, piggeries, poultry farms and kitchen gardens, while for many years the Tregenna Castle at St Ives had its own Jersey herd. Along with the great companies were the minnows; the Snowdon Mountain Hotels & Tramroad Company, for example, which was also active in the refreshment room business, opened its own small hostelry in 1896 on the summit of Snowdon Mountain, besides taking a lease of two very reputable hotels near Llanberis in the valley below. But, great or small, they were subject to human shortcomings. In April 1911 the *Daily Mail* reported the case of the doctor from Ulster who had journeyed to Glasgow the previous Christmas Eve, spending the night at the Caledonian's Central Hotel. There he requested a morning call in time for the only train to Arbroath, where he was to assist in an operation, but the staff must have been affected by the Christmas spirit for the call never came, and when the good doctor finally reached Arbroath the operation was over. The fate of the patient is not recorded, but the doctor sued the Caledonian for the sum of five guineas – and lost.

World War I had a massive effect on lifestyles and social attitudes everywhere and the railway hotels, very firmly rooted in Victorian traditions, were not best placed to adjust. There was a growing capacity and demand for leisure; the emphasis now shifted away from the city centres and the railways looked for existing rural properties to add to their empires. In 1919 the Great Eastern took over the very prestigious Felix at Felixstowe. By 1929 the Great Western, always the most cautious in the hotel trade, had acquired the Manor House near Moretonhampstead on Dartmoor, a fine mock-Jacobean mansion built some 20 years earlier for Viscount Hambledon, chairman of W. H. Smith. In 1931 it was the turn of the LMS, which had bought the former country home of historian George Trevelyan near Stratford-on-Avon and named it the Welcombe Hotel. The Welcombe lay somewhat close to GWR territory, and in its first summer the LMS directors were particularly keen to bring London clients to their hotel on their own rail services. Their journey lay from Euston down the West Coast Main Line as far as Blisworth in Northamptonshire, junction for the old Stratford-on-Avon & Midland Junction Railway, one of those sleepy lines that used to wander impecuniously across the Midland shires. At Blisworth, hotel guests would exchange their Euston express for the 'Ro-Railer', a remarkable single-decker bus with both rail and road wheels. Then off would go this contraption on its 40-mile trundle past the cows and distant signals of deepest England, to the goods yard at Stratford where, as if itself in need of a drink after its tiring journey, it heaved itself from the line and headed off along the road to the Welcombe.

A rather different leisure venture by the LMS was its holiday camp at Prestatyn, on the North Wales Coast, opened in 1939 as a joint venture with travel magnates Thomas Cook. Holiday camps before the War attracted a much wider social range than they do now, and in that last summer before Hitler struck it was a common sight to see doctors and solicitors chatting beside the chlorinated swimming pool or sipping cocktails at the 'Prestatyn Clipper' bar. But in general the 1930s were a time of depression in industry and rationalisation in business. Once-great hotels, such as the North Western in Liverpool and the Cannon Street in London, were closed and converted into offices, while it was a particularly sad day when the Midland Grand at St Pancras also succumbed. The trouble there was not only the 'de-gentrification' of the area, but the massive cost of bringing the hotel up-to-date. As LMS chairman Lord Stamp remarked, 'It is impossible to put in a new piece of heating apparatus, or anything of that kind without meeting the same obstacles that would be encountered in modifying the Rock of Gibraltar.'

The shortage of funds affecting all the railways meant that the large-scale rebuilding, which Victorian hotels needed if they were to compete, was usually not forthcoming. But one exception was the Queens in Leeds, where the old structure dating back to 1863 was knocked down and a very handsome brand-new 200-bedroom edifice opened in 1937. This hotel, recognisable today as a particularly fine example of its period, was the first hotel in Britain to be fully air-conditioned; outside, the Leeds Corporation Tramways slewed its tramlines away from the hotel and installed special noise-deadened points to increase the comfort of guests – a nice tribute from one form of transport to another. But Leeds apart, it was a policy of 'holding the line' at the city hotels – a policy not altogether regretted by some, who formed a nostalgic attachment to places that had been a landmark in the local community for generations.

World War II had a much more direct effect upon hotel life than the first, for apart from manpower shortages and changed lifestyles there was the target presented to the Luftwaffe by large buildings in city centres. Over a score of railway hotels suffered bomb damage to some extent. London fared the worst, though as luck would have it, the three totally destroyed by enemy action had all been previously converted to offices – Cannon Street and Holborn Viaduct, mentioned above, and the old Terminus Hotel at London Bridge, bought by the railway for office use as far back as 1893. As well as air raids, there was the effect of friendly 'invasion' in the form of requisitioning for

War Casualty: the 1867 City Terminus (later Cannon Street) Hotel, designed by E. M. Barry (who also designed the Charing Cross Hotel), was destroyed in a 1941 air raid. *Illustrated London News.*

military hostels, hospitals and training centres. These takeovers, which in some cases lasted two or three years after the end of hostilities, particularly affected the port and coastal centres, and normal life in all the South Coast hotels came to a complete halt in 1944 as the build-up to D-day began. Those that did remain open were havens of civility in a country on the rack. When Lord Mountbatten's destroyer HMS *Kelly* was torpedoed in the North Sea, and was towed to Tyneside over four days and nights, barely afloat and half her crew dead or injured, Mountbatten headed for landfall at the Royal Station Hotel in Newcastle. 'I went as I was,' he recorded in his diary for 13 May 1940, 'no luggage, unshaven and filthy, to the Station Hotel and after 91 hours in tow a real bed was heaven.'

The official booklet *British Railways in Peace and War*, published 1944, quotes the following statistics:

Hotels owned and managed by the railways	53
Hotels owned but let	16
Hotels closed due to war conditions	3
Hotels requisitioned	14
Damaged by air attack	23

The bulk of those in the last two categories were in London or on the coasts and some of those, when they finally reopened after the war, were never to be the same again. The social trends of the inter-war years had accelerated enormously and the railway companies, as the war receded, looked to invest what money they had in hotels for new markets. The Great Western now took over the Grand Pump Room in Bath, while the Southern broke entirely new ground in South Devon, where it purchased the splendid Knowle at Sidmouth. If the intention was to add a little spice to an ultra-respectable hotel chain, the Knowle was a good choice because the original part of the building had been designed in 1805 for Sir Francis Dashwood, founder of the Hell Fire Club, notorious in history for its wickedness and debauchery.

The Nationalisation of railways in 1948 put an early end to these attempts at expansion, for there now came into being a Hotels Executive responsible for all the hotels and for all railway catering as well. This Executive is discussed more fully in Chapter 7, but its most significant feature was that hotels and catering were now expected to pay their way, taking one year

EAT CENTRAL HOTEL, THE WINTER GARDENS.

The Winter Gardens were a highlight of the former Great Central Hotel. Well-known as '222 Marylebone Road', the British Railways Headquarters for 40 years, it may soon entertain hotel guests once more. *G. Gundry collection.*

with another. Ironically, the Executive made its headquarters at the former Great Central Hotel at Marylebone – a place which along with its sister the Victoria in Nottingham, had been planned by the Great Central Railway on opening its main line to London in 1899, but which in the event was built privately by Sir John Blundell Maple because the GCR had run out of funds. With its magnificent palm court and (in the early years) its cycle track on the roof, the Great Central was bought by the LNER for office conversion in 1946 and now found itself the nerve centre of much of the British Railways empire.

Dug in at '222 Marylebone Road,' as it now was, the accountants of the Hotels Executive cast an extremely beady eye upon each hotel. In the next six years no fewer than 13 were sold, including Sidmouth after a life in railway ownership of just four years. The cost of bringing the remaining buildings up-to-date was soon to be the death-knell of several more, for not only was the market changing to the business conference and the car-borne tourist, it was becoming more demanding, with central heating and hot and cold water in all bedrooms expected as a matter of course. At the same time, tighter fire regulations meant more doors, exits and fittings. To add to these problems, the city centre sites which had once been prime assets were rapidly becoming a liability. The age of road transport had brought with it problems of traffic noise, while other buildings clustering round severely limited essential car parking space and, indeed, modern extensions of any kind. The new hotels that were springing up on the outskirts of towns suffered none of these problems.

British Transport Hotels, in facing this mounting crisis, had ever since 1948 been hampered by the terms of its existence which restricted it to sites closely associated with the railway network. However in 1968 the Old Course Hotel at St Andrews, the first new railway hotel for 30 years, was opened on the site of the former engine sheds there, and that same year a new Transport Act seemed to hold out promise of much greater things by abolishing the old constraint and empowering the British Railways Board to provide hotels in any part of Britain – 'and, with the Minister's consent, elsewhere.' But the Old Course was destined to be the last railway hotel of all. The 1970 election returned a Conservative government, which refused to allow BTH to go ahead with well-advanced plans for a new hotel at Gatwick, and amid much chagrin the mirage of a new golden age faded away.

The steady decline of the hotels empire was mirrored by the number of hotels owned. In 1901, the number had stood at 61 (including those owned by the railways but operated by a variety of contract holders). Thirty years later, at the zenith of their empire, the figure stood at 78. In 1961 it had fallen to 37, and in 1981, just before the final break-up, to 29. All the hotels in these latter days were the better-known and more profitable establishments, but even some of these were now being left behind by events. Some cities, like Liverpool, had been savagely hit by Britain's industrial decline and could no longer support the way of life for which the hotels had catered, while at places like Derby and Sheffield, the centre of gravity of the town had moved away, leaving the hotels in unattractive, run-down areas.

The problems were just as severe for those sold off into private ownership. Some, like Sidmouth, Felixstowe and Preston, were converted into offices, while others, like the Sandringham at Hunstanton and the South Eastern at Deal, struggled on in an atmosphere of growing mustiness and decay. Parts of these places were let off as flats and there were attempts to open modish restaurants to attract local trade. But there were fires caused by old wiring, soaring costs and ever-diminishing trade, leading eventually, inevitably, to demolition gangs' hammers.

But the Victorian scale and style which was such a headache to the operator was starting to become by the 1970s a public attraction in itself. Victoriana was returning to fashion with a vengeance, nowhere more so than among the high-spending American tourists now flocking to Britain. London hotels like the Great Western Royal at Paddington and the Charing Cross were becoming Meccas for dollar-rich visitors, while others like the Welcombe at Stratford, the Royal Station at York and the Gleneagles offered an ideal base for history-minded tourists. Refurbishment would attract a still bigger clientele, but without the money to prime the pump the situation remained deadlocked.

Against this challenging background, the organisation of British Transport Hotels in the 1970s was completely changed. Since Nationalisation, the company had run by Areas – London & South, North Western & Midland, Eastern, and Scotland. These Areas were first reduced to three, and then replaced in 1979 by functional Divisions – City Hotels, Leisure Hotels, and the optimistically-named Investment Hotels, which had the biggest question marks over them. Into this new set-up was brought the Grosvenor Hotel at Victoria in London, which had been leased out continuously from 1899 to 1977. The philosophy applied to this long-lost prodigal was refreshingly businesslike; identify the market, plan a hotel to meet it and put all resources into realising the plan. The market, in the teeming tourist environs of Victoria, was indentified as no higher than three-star standard, with self-service continental breakfast packs placed in each bedroom and a coffee-house style restaurant with a maximum of help-yourself service. The tired interior of the Grosvenor was transformed, fresh paint appeared in every hall and room and within two years the hotel was the most profitable of the 29-strong BTH chain.

A crowning event for railway hotels in 1977 was the British Open Golf Championship, held for the first time on BTH territory – the Ailsa course at Turnberry. No lover of the game will readily forget the scene as the giants of the day, Tom Watson and Jack Nicklaus of the United States, fought it out stroke for stroke down the final nine holes, until in the shadow of the great hotel and in front of a television audience of millions, Watson holed out to clinch the match by one stroke on the eighteenth. It was, they say, possibly the finest finish in the history of the Open. In that great boardroom in the sky, the directors of the old Glasgow & South Western Railway must have been rubbing their hands with glee.

Sadly, these successes were to be the swansong of the railway hotels, for the General Election of 1979 brought in a Government intent on privatising all possible state assets. The writing was now on the wall and in 1981 Gleneagles, along with the Caledonian and North British in Edinburgh, were sold to form Gleneagles Hotels plc. In 1982, the Midland in Derby and the Victoria in Sheffield followed into another small private company, while the Old Course at St Andrews went as a 'one-off.' The big sale came in 1983, with 21 of the remaining 23 hotels sold in batches to various owners. Early in 1984 the North British in Glasgow followed, and the last, the Queens in Leeds, went to Trust House Forte that June.

Thus ended nearly a century and a half of railway-owned hotels – an era of magnificence, a story of the great names of architecture and cuisine, and a mirror of the social history of Britain at the zenith of her power. In one chapter it is quite impossible to do more than sketch the briefest outline of that story. But to conclude, let us quote a writer in *Country Life* in 1937, who, commenting on the heyday of the railway hotels from what was then a modern standpoint, observed:

> 'It was not exactly that the Station Hotels were exclusive, but there were certainly people who were very much at their ease in them, and there were classes who would never have dreamt of using them even for light refreshment.'

Forty years on, with the end in sight, that was still true; it was their essence, their strength, and maybe at the last, their weakness.

5
Take it Away

Though early railway travel was a hungry and tiring business indeed, not every traveller wanted a full meal or a night's rest, and of course in the days of 'refreshment stops' there was time only for the most hurried of snacks. As *The Railway Traveller's Handybook* of 1862 put it:

> 'As there are usually some two or three hundred persons requiring refreshments, and only about a dozen hands to supply them . . . we shall advise the railway traveller to take his refreshment with him.'

Not everyone found it convenient to follow this advice and the hawkers and peddlers, whom we met in the first chapter, continued to do good business despite injunctions against the nuisance and delay they caused. There was obviously a big gap in the market for mobile picnics, and it was not surprising to find once again those entrepreneurs *par excellence*, Messrs Spiers and Pond, filling it. Their idea, first put into practice in the summer of 1871, was to hire out food baskets from the refreshment rooms they managed on the Midland Railway; passengers would consume the contents leaving the basket itself, with its dirty crockery, to be collected by station staff further down the line.

It was not long before the Midland Railway itself realised the potential of the scheme. On 1 March 1875 its energetic hotel and catering manager, William Towle, began his own luncheon basket service, based at Derby station. The baskets themselves were like miniature wicker hampers, similar to the Victorian family picnic baskets, and the advertisement shows two 'classes' available, at 3s 0d (15p) and 2s 0d (10p). Baskets quickly became popular on all the major lines, and the railways soon found it necessary to fix an enamel plate to each basket, signifying its owner, home station, and identification number.

As the popularity of the baskets grew, so the variety of their

A typical lunchbasket, with contents (more generous and appetising than usual in this publicity photograph!), and a copy of William Towle's first advertisement for this service in 1875. *Travellers Fare.*

contents increased. Austin Brereton in his *Transport* magazine feature of July 1902 mentions the Highland Railway's 'Kingussie' breakfast basket, with no fewer than 10,000 in one season sold from Perth, Inverness, Kyle of Lochalsh, and a handful of smaller stations including Kingussie itself. Down at the other extremity of Britain, Brereton describes the scene at one of Spiers & Pond's refreshment rooms on the South Eastern Railway:

'They make a special feature of the sale of tea baskets at Dover, where they have two bars, specially built on the pier, for the purpose. These bars are fitted with special Geyser boilers, for the supply of boiling water. Ten boys in uniform are kept in readiness for serving the tea baskets in the train to the passengers arriving from the Continent. In addition, hot "Oxo" is also sold.'

Such beverages must have been very welcome after a couple of hours on the cold and windswept deck of a crowded channel steamer.

The most popular service remained the midday luncheon basket, and a system developed whereby passengers' orders were telegraphed ahead and the baskets put aboard at various points. It was a great excitement for children to see the 'nippers,' as the refreshment room boys were known, holding up the laden baskets and calling out the passengers' names. Sometimes, if there was a rush of business, the refreshment rooms could not cope and basketless passengers were left anxiously hoping that their particular orders had been passed on to the next stopping point.

A basket lunch usually consisted of cold viands, salad with a roll and butter, and something to drink. A 1876 London & North Western tariff from Chester station offered 'The Aristocrat' at 5s 0d (25p) with chicken, ham or tongue, bread, cheese, and either a full pint of claret or *half a pint* of sherry (a weaker brew, surely, than that we know today!) At 2s 6d (12½p) there was 'The Democrat': cold meat or pie, bread and cheese, with a pint bottle of ale or stout. In 1884 the enterprising Midland Railway announced a 'hot basket', available at Derby and Leicester, containing steak or chop with vegetables, cheese, bread, and half a bottle of claret, stout, appollinaris or aerated water. Not much seems to have been recorded about the success or otherwise of keeping this collation hot! It may well have been the difficulties of managing such a meal on one's knee that prompted the historian Acworth, in his *Railways of England* (1889), to observe:

'Some English railways might do worse than make trial of the German transportable *Spieseplatten*, or tray with legs, in place of luncheon baskets. "Non omnia possumus omnes" and it is not given to everyone to balance a mutton chop and potatoes gracefully on his knee, the while he pours himself out a glass of claret with his hands.'

Acworth's plea was taken seriously by the Great Northern Railway at least, for an old photograph published 1902 shows a lady with upon her knee a basket, inscribed 'GNR – Peterboro', supported at the back by a spindly pair of folding wooden legs. These legs look very much as if they could get broken or fold up at the wrong moment, and therein may lie the reason why this idea never really caught on.

The basket business reached its peak about the turn of the century, when dining cars were still rather few and far between. The London & North Western Railway in 1906 advertised the service from 22 of its biggest stations, with hot lunch baskets at five of the most strategic places – Preston, Crewe, Rugby, Stafford, and Northampton – where passengers were most likely to be changing trains with insufficient time for a hot meal. But the system was hardly foolproof and the tea baskets, in particular, were difficult to regulate well. A train delayed, and all the waiting teas would go cold and stewed. A sudden surge of business, and agitated passengers would demand to know why their baskets were not ready immediately. A contemporary writer in *Truth* magazine catalogues a 'shillingsworth' tea-basket from Rugby: one pot of tea, 'insufficiently hot but unnecessarily strong', a small open jug of tepid water, small portions of milk and sugar, two flimsy slices of bread and butter, two hunks of plum cake 'of the common or school-treat variety,' and one small stick of chocolate – total value, 'possibly 4½d.' 'According to my experience,' the writer remarks, 'Rugby does not differ much in the matter of tea-baskets from other stations north, south, east, and west. On a recent occasion . . . the tea was served in a pot with a broken spout, and I had to drink it out of a cup badly chipped about the edges, and to stir it with an extremely dirty spoon.' With the handling and treatment teabaskets must have received, damaged crockery must have been only too common; certainly no such system would pass the scrutiny of today's environmental health officers.

There were attempts also to increase the spend and hence the profitability involved in baskets. Then as now this was a challenge constantly facing caterers, and then as now it aroused public ire. The *Tourist* magazine for July 1903 passes

> 'a word on the Great Northern Railway tea basket; tea and two slices of bread and butter (6d) is not value for money; a slice of cake could well be added and would result in a demand for tea baskets that would astonish the purveyors, but no! This is not their way, they prefer to add a pretty basket of chocolate biscuits, and charge another sixpence.'

The value of baskets was always in question, for a very adequate dining car meal could often be obtained for the same price.

The quality of the food itself did not escape criticism. Like school dinners, the list of chops, cold meats, salads and wine sounded all right on paper, but hurried preparation and indifferent ingredients too often produced an unappetising repast. The situation was summed up by an LNWR traffic apprentice of 1912 who, parodying Omar Khayyam, delivered himself thus, under the head of '3s 6d!!':

> A Loaf of Bread, a Cup of Wine, and thou
> Beside me on the cushion, and I trow
> The Railway train is paradise enow.
>
> When from old age she's disinclined to lay,
> The hen from earth is quickly called away;
> Whither her Spirit goes I cannot say.
>
> But this I know, if anyone should ask it,
> Her body, or as poets say, her 'casket'
> Reposes in the Railway Luncheon Basket.
>
> Behold the leg that wandered once at will,
> With some pin feathers clinging to it still;
> How thin it looks bedecked with paper frill.
>
> The breast, unruffled now by love or care,
> Looks keen and sharp when of its plumage bare;
> 'Twill cut your fingers if you don't take care.
>
> Now she will quickly travel down the line,
> Companioned by a bottle of bad wine,
> And doubtful slice of ham, cut very fine.
>
> And, if for further luxuries you seek,
> A piece of cheese, decidedly antique,
> And roll that's left the oven for a week.
>
> Come, traveller, undo the basket's strap,
> And place the savoury mess upon your lap;
> You have my sympathy, my poor, dear chap.
>
> For if upon the ancient bird you dine,
> Or finish up that dose of shilling wine,
> You have a keener appetite than mine.

Despite such strictures, meal baskets remained an everyday part of railway travel for many more years and it was only with the advent of buffet cars in the early 1930s that the writing appeared on the wall. As late as March 1940, a GWR tariff advertised a 3s 0d (15p) basket containing cold chicken (leg) and ham with bread, butter, margarine and cheese, while for an

A tea wagon at Euston about 1904, with its urn simmering over its spirit lamp, Bath buns open to the air, and tea baskets belonging to both Euston and Rugby. *Travellers Fare*.

A rather more elaborate trolley at Derby in February 1908; attendant Frank Torrington (later of the Midland Hotel) is backed by a splendid array of period notices and advertisements. *Crown Copyright. National Railway Museum, York*.

extra sixpence (2½p) the chicken joint would be wing or breast.
A footnote adds that 'one one-sixth ounce pat of butter is served,
supplemented with margarine.' But worsening shortages of food
and staff meant that the end was nigh, and early in 1941 the
lunchbasket system ceased, on the GWR and elsewhere, for
good.

Throughout the life of the baskets the railways were plagued
with problems of losses and breakage. The GWR Hotels and
Catering handbook in the 1930s carried the note: 'In view of the
serious losses by breakage and otherwise of Basket fittings, the
company venture to solicit the co-operation of passengers to
ensure their proper use, and to replace them in the Baskets
when finished with.' As always with notices like this, the people
who read them were those who treated the baskets properly in
any case, and carelessness and dishonesty by the rough and the
wicked continued to take their toll. The cost of staff employed in
delivering the baskets and collecting 'empties' represented a
further drawback, and after the first War the companies began

to cast around for some cheap and disposable means of packing a light meal. The GWR came up with its Light Lunch Box, made of waxed cardboard, which for 1s 3d (6p) offered the passenger sandwiches, cake and fruit. Later, as cheap unbreakable plastic trays became available, the service spread to cold tray meals, sold in boxes called 'Compakt' or some such snazzy, phonetic name beloved of the advertising world. This service was particularly popular with parties. Both packed and tray meals are services that continue, albeit patchily advertised, to this day. In 1985 the wheel turned a complete circle when the Station Hotel at Inverness, by then in private hands, began selling breakfast packs for passengers on the overnight sleeper trains to the south, thus competing with Travellers-Fare breakfasts sold in London refreshment rooms!

Both baskets and boxes were on sale in their heyday not only from refreshment rooms but also from platform trolleys. These trolleys were a natural means of taking the food on large stations to the customer, instead of expecting the customer to go looking for the food. It was another method of alleviating the notorious overcrowding in refreshment rooms, a need exemplified by a writer in the *Daily Chronicle* of 20 July 1907, who exhorted refreshment staff thus:

> 'Have the tea ready! At large centres, such say, as Cambridge, Oxford, Rugby, etc, it is difficult to get a cup of tea by those who cannot leave their carriages. If the caterers are wise they will offer their page boys a premium on all they sell.'

The trolleys were the ideal answer to this plea, for by operating along the platforms they were able to refresh passengers through the train windows. Passengers soon learned not to give a £1 note if the train were about to pull out, for trolley attendants could be mysteriously slow fumbling for change on such occasions. Only in recent years, with air-conditioned carriages with sealed windows and with buffets on most expresses, has this service become nigh extinct.

Some of these trolleys were quite elaborate affairs carrying a range of provender; others were more basic 'tea wagons', which in the days before insulated containers carried an urn heated by a spirit lamp, so that a freshly made pot was always to hand. Even more basic were the 'usherette' style baskets slung round the

When this period picture was taken at Paddington early in 1939, platform trolleys were soon to disappear as a wartime economy. *Travellers Fare.*

vendor's neck, offering sandwiches, buns and sweets.

During World War II the trolleys went into store so as to yield up their vital manpower, but to maintain some sort of service and help out the hard-pressed refreshment rooms the LMSR in 1943 introduced the idea of Railbars. These pre-fabricated plywood light refreshment kiosks were assembled on site on pre-cast concrete bases (supply of the plywood having been agreed by the Ministry of Works and Planning). They were extremely light and could be put together very quickly by unskilled labour; staff on windy platforms often feared the whole contraption would take off into the sky at any moment. These railbars did yeoman service for many years; their name continued in use for small tea bars until quite recently, by which time it had become somewhat confusing, leading travellers to believe, wrongly, that the premises were licensed.

The railbar idea was taken a stage further in the 1950s when two road vans were fitted out as mobile refreshment rooms. They were useful when proper buffets were closed for rebuilding, or at special railway 'outside events' such as depot open days; but there were limits here, for since Nationalisation railway

The platform vendor was still plying his trade after World War II, as in this photograph at King's Cross in 1953. *BR/OPC*.

PLEASE PUT EMPTY CARTONS, WASTE PAPER, ETC. IN THE NEAREST LITTER BASKET.

catering has been restricted by statute to trading on railway-owned land.

But taking refreshments on trolleys to the passengers rather than the other way round was obviously good business sense, and the train catering operators began to take a serious interest in it in the late 1940s, when post-war shortages were making full restaurant car meals very difficult. They were very much constrained by the narrow train corridors. On the continent, on-train trolleys had long been commonplace, but continental railways have a wider loading gauge than in Britain – ie tunnels, overbridges and lineside structures give a wider clearance – and their coach bodies are that much wider, roundly 9in–1ft. The extra few inches make all the difference; in Britain, the battle to bring in on-train trolleys resulted in a series of false starts stretching over nearly forty years.

Old photographs show a tall and rickety-looking trolley being manoeuvred down the side corridors of a compartment-stock express as early as 1948, and on 8 April 1949 the magazine

Caterer & Hotelkeeper reported Lord Inman, newly-appointed Chairman of British Transport Hotels, as promising that 'food trolleys were to be introduced on all lines to serve snacks in the corridors.' Problems struck immediately. The trolleys were so narrow as to be unwieldy and top-heavy; worse, whenever there were standing passengers or luggage in the corridors, they could make no progress at all. Passengers and staff alike complained, and Lord Inman was obliged to let the scheme drop and re-think the matter.

By 1960 there had been something of a move towards open saloon rolling stock, in place of the compartment style, and this seemed to offer more room for manoeuvre. Accordingly a London Midland Region press release of 28 November 1960 promised that 'specially-constructed trolleys will be available on 53 London Midland services, from today.' But once again plans rapidly came unstuck. There was indeed more room for the attendant to operate, but the problems of stacked luggage

An early corridor trolley in experimental service, on the North Eastern Region of the newly-formed British Railways, in 1948. *British Rail.*

remained. Custom from passengers was rather slow – many people wanted a beer or whisky, but as each individual catering car was in those days licensed to sell liquor only within its own confines, the trolleys could not oblige.

The staff were not fully behind the scheme – there was a feeling that trolleys discouraged passengers from going along to the buffet car where they would probably have spent more. Furthermore, guards and ticket collectors still had difficulty squeezing past the trolleys to carry out their duties, and claimed that the trolleys constituted a hazard in case of emergency. The upshot was that the National Union of Railwaymen refused to co-operate in any more such schemes until substantial changes were made to trolleys and rolling stock.

Meanwhile, trolley services of a rather different kind were operating on some cross-country and 'dated' trains, that is trains which run for a part of the year only, such as the summer holiday period. These trains have never justified the expense of buffet cars which would stand idle the rest of the year. That there was a demand for refreshments on board was obvious, so local agreements were struck whereby the refreshment room side of the business filled a trolley which was based in the train's brake van, venturing out down the train if and when conditions allowed. To man these services, the refreshment rooms employed all manner of railway staff anxious to earn a bit of spare cash on their days off, plus, in the summer peak, a number of 'casuals' and students as well. A valued service was being provided without doubt, but the combination of dingy brake van, limited supplies and unskilled staff often gave the operation a somewhat unprofessional air.

At one time, one of these services consisted merely of an open-topped wicker hamper on wheels, towed along by a rope – certainly a 'minimum-overheads' approach. But in the 1960s a portable buffet counter was devised, permitting a bay of an open saloon coach to be used for refreshment selling, and this paved the way for the mini-buffet scheme which came to fruition in 1980. By this time, a number of buffet cars on London area outer-surburban services were life-expired, and in the straitened economy of the times replacement was impossible. One seating bay plus the adjacent toilet was removed from a number of saloon vehicles, and a trolley was designed to lock into position in the resulting space. The attendant loaded this trolley

A part-timer loads his wares into the brake van of a Manchester – North Wales summer season train at Stockport, *circa* 1970. *D. Birch.*

at the station depot, wheeled it on board using a special ramp, unloading it again at the scheduled station which could well be short of the train's destination if business were light beyond that point. Here was the key to flexible, low-cost catering on short-distance or lightly-loaded trains, and the principle has now spread widely throughout the country.

The sight of trolleys re-appearing on trains in whatever form was bound to raise the old question of mobile or 'ambulant' trolleys afresh, and this was lent new weight by the drive to establish upmarket 'Executive' services on Inter-City routes. The latest Mk III rolling stock was now offering maximum gangway width and, more important, much greater luggage space, along with automatic vestibule doors. With these improvements, the National Union of Railwaymen first agreed to operate trolleys in first class vehicles, which have wider gangways, and then in 1984 the union agreed to operate throughout the train. The impact on the level of service offered the passengers, and hence on public opinion, was immediate.

This new world of on-train trolleys called for a radical new design, and the lessons of 30-odd years before were recalled. Heavy insulated hot water urns, for instance, may be fine perched atop a platform trolley, but on the narrow train version they had proved to be the prime cause of top-heaviness and trouble. So the new trolleys had their tanks lower down, with the water raised to tap level by carbon dioxide pressure, like keg beer. If left too long, however, this gas will dissolve slightly in water, so the attendant has to be careful not to serve passengers with fizzy, tepid tea!

While the trolley saga was gradually resolving itself, the various railways had turned at various times to automatic vending machines as a means of filling the gap. Penny-in-the-slot chocolate machines had been part and parcel of the station concourse scene for generations, but in 1931 the Great Western Railway took the step of installing one in the Paddington–Weston-Super-Mare express. But almost immediately problems arose. The machine – a straightforward mechanical one – did not take kindly to the motion of the train and tended to jam.

An automatic machine, known as a 'Chocolate Boy', installed in a Paddington – Weston-super-Mare express, January 1931, *BBC Hulton Picture Library.*

On-train staff, busy with other duties elsewhere, were loath to go and wrestle with it, whereupon passengers thumped it, which sometimes did the trick, and sometimes not. The omens for this particular experiment seemed not very good.

By the 1960s technology had moved a long way and new experiments were begun. This time, the electric power supply used for train heating was tapped, but this current is seldom absolutely constant. As the new machines were sensitive to such variation, breakdowns were once again the order the day. Further, a new threat had emerged on the train – the football hooligan shod in 'bovver boots.' Suffice it to say that the saga of automatic vending on trains is, as modern parlance has it, 'on-going.'

Vending on station platforms by contrast has proved much more worthwhile. Station vending generally backs up other, staffed, catering units. The machines ease the load at peak periods, and they come into their own late in the evening and early in the morning when the staff are off duty. They can, however, if all is not well, take a traveller's money while witholding his snack, something which has been known to produce quite alarming rage and fulminations in disappointed passengers. This hazard is one reason why complete banks of automatic machines forming an auto-buffet, like one that operated at Blackpool Central in the 1960s, have never become widespread. Economic and space-saving they may be, but the more they vend, the higher the stakes when something goes wrong.

Neither is there great solace in the machines fitted with a 'voice chip', which appeared at one or two stations in London quite recently. These machines would suddenly inform the startled customers 'Your drink is on its way.' If a certain drink were out of stock, it would recommend another selection; as they turned to go, it bade them have a nice day. But when it was out of order and a helpful voice was most needed it remained by definition, 'mum.' Unkind souls said that it had learnt the trick by watching railway platform staff at work. The old-fashioned human tea-lady and her modern successor have much in their favour.

6
Hard Times

World War I, the greatest holocaust yet faced by mankind, was arguably the greatest agent of social change ever seen – the cataclysms of more recent years included. Consciously or not, the nations went to war hungry for change. In Britain the long Victorian high summer and the Edwardian autumn were over, and the social order which had sustained them and in turn been sustained by them was about to be broken for ever. No-one could have quite forseen the scale of technical development the Great War was also to produce. Together, these changes were to have deep and permanent effect upon railways everywhere, and in Britain, where the railway network was oldest-established, that effect was the most profound.

With the first bursts of gunfire in that momentous August of 1914 the Government took direct control of the British railway system, for the carriage of troops, munitions, and war supplies now demanded top priority. Restaurant car services, with their high proportion of male staff, were at once depleted by the departure of large numbers of men to put on the King's uniform. Even so, a fair number managed to continue throughout the war, particularly on the Midland, Great Central, and London & South Western Railways, while Pullman on the Brighton and the South Eastern lines also kept several services going. Refreshment rooms, where most of the staff were women and girls, were less affected, and one or two now carved a hallowed niche in the nation's memory. For countless thousands of British Tommies, the Long Bar at London's Victoria station was the last rendezvous with their loved ones, as to the popular strain 'Goodby-ee' they boarded the troop trains to Dover, Flanders, and all too often oblivion.

After the end of hostilities in 1918, railway catering was soon on its way back to normal, but now the deep changes wrought by the War began to make themselves felt, and the most immediate of these was the coming-of-age of motor transport. Before 1914, cars, lorries and buses had by and large been expensive, primitive, and less than fully reliable. Four years later, toughened by the demands of war and produced on a massive scale, they had been transformed into a practical means of transport in every way, and were set to become an essential part of civilian daily life. The great demobilisation of 1918–19 now brought onto the market tens of thousands of men looking for work, and with them fleets of fully serviceable army surplus vans and lorries. Discharged soldiers bought surplus vehicles in great numbers, and the age of the bus company and the road haulier was well and truly launched. Britain's railways were about to lose for ever their monopoly of transport.

But for a time these clouds seemed to threaten only the furthest-flung and least profitable branches. The main lines, soon to be consolidated under the Grouping of 1923, continued to thrive. It was the age of the Great Expresses – the Flying Scotsman, the Royal Scot, the Irish Mail, the Cornish Riviera – all, of course, with dining cars. In the year 1925, passengers on British trains consumed between them over 7½ million meals, into which went 965 tons of meat, 848 tons of bread and 779 tons of fish. Multiple sittings of meals were the rule, and the chief steward, passing through the train handing out reservation tickets for first, second and third sitting, was a familiar sight.

No railway is more fondly remembered for its dining car services between the wars than the Great Western – the holiday line to the West Country. After its comparatively late start this company's catering had settled down to a consistently high standard, and travellers off on their holidays were in the mood to enjoy it. The snag was that on summer weekends in July and August, when the holiday traffic rose to its peak, there were just not enough restaurant cars and crews for all the special trains needed. The GWR made the most of its resources by sending down a complete train of restaurant cars from Paddington to Newton Abbot on Friday evenings, stocked up ready to work returning services the following day. This meant the London crews travelling down with their vehicles, lodging overnight in Newton Abbot. Sometimes 'digs' were available, but more often they ended up sleeping in railway offices or even on the cars themselves – hardly the best preparation for a long and gruelling spell on duty on the Saturday!

In its quest for passenger comfort, the Great Western at this time built two pairs of articulated dining cars with an early form of air-conditioning that relied on wet ice for cooling. This novel system, which seems to have been only moderately effective, proved horrendously expensive to operate, requiring the supply of very nearly *one ton* of ice to each set each day. These cars operated for many years on the South Wales route, but as time went on, the air-conditioning proved less and less reliable and passengers increasingly found it to be 'not in operation.'

Another novely that proved a mixed blessing was Nigel Gresley's well-known quintuple articulated dining car set, built for the Great Northern Railway in 1921. The idea was that as five catering vehicles would always be needed together on a busy service (in this case King's Cross to the West Riding) their intermediate ends could be mounted upon common bogies, saving expense and weight. But a mechanical defect in any one of the cars meant of course that all five had to be taken out of the train, seriously disrupting both seating and catering, to the chagrin of railway and restaurant car staff.

Passengers, too, had good reason to be wary of the 'Quint' set and the train in which it worked. The 10.10am from King's Cross, loaded to 14 coaches, was booked to detach first a Hull portion at Doncaster, and then a Bradford portion at Wakefield; the main portion including the 'Quint' went through to Leeds, whence yet another portion went on to Harrogate. Now each of these portions perforce had its own brake van, and the 'Quint' included two. This meant that Hull passengers, travelling at the rear from King's Cross, were obliged to pick their way through the swaying corridors of no fewer than eleven vehicles to get to the dining cars, negotiating on the way as many as four brake vans which in those days would be piled high with luggage, mailbags and fish boxes. Nor was this all. By the time one had struggled through to the diner, had a meal and struggled back, it was by no means unknown to find that one's own portion of the train, complete with luggage, had been detached at Doncaster or Wakefield ... The 'Quint' was thus often an enemy of passengers and staff alike, and we shall meet it again before the end of this book.

Over on the Southern Railway with its shorter distances travellers and caterers encountered no such hazards. Much of the catering was still contracted out to Spiers & Pond; in 1930 this changed (as it did in the refreshment rooms) to Frederick Hotels. On the South Eastern and Brighton lines, it remained in the hands of Pullman, usually with supplementary charge. This no doubt reflected the affluence of the area, and the distinctive Pullman dining car marshalled into a train of green Southern passenger coaches remained a familiar sight on those lines until well after Nationalisation. Some of the Pullmans were non-supplement cars for fluid dining purposes, particularly on South Eastern services.

But the pride of the country in the inter-war years was surely the Flying Scotsman, from 1928 non-stop between King's Cross and Edinburgh. The locomotive had a corridor tender, allowing driver and fireman to walk through and be relieved by a fresh crew en route, no doubt much to the surprise of passengers sitting in the front coach! Passengers enjoyed a cocktail bar, hairdressing saloon, and ladies' retiring room; newsboys sold

LMS chairman Sir Josiah Stamp inspects his company's first buffet car at Euston on 2 June 1932. The contraption on the counter, looking rather like an old-fashioned beer pump, is a cork remover. *BBC Hulton Picture Library.*

magazines, and later there was a wireless and gramophone service relayed by earphones to first class seats. The ratio of staff to passengers was enormous – and so were the costs – but in those days when the railway monopoly still held good for long-distance travel, this mattered little. The LNER summed it all up in a delightful period poster which showed the figure of that great traveller, Dr Samuel Johnson, relaxing in a Scotland-bound diner and, claret in hand, declaring to his companion:

> The Doctor said to Boswell, 'Sir,
> It seemeth plain to me
> That the obvious route to Scotland
> Is from King's Cross, LNE.'

It was the Great Depression which began suddenly and catastrophically late in 1929 and sent its long shadow far into the following decade, that caused the traveller's purse to become rather less well-lined, and the railway caterers to cast about for ways of meeting a new and slimmer market. The buffet car plans of thirty years before, which had been seen off on the Great Central by a suspicious and conservative public, were therefore

This combined buffet-restaurant car served snacks and light meals on the GWR from 1938. Note the careful posing of this publicity shot, with the models (probably head office staff) and the cardboard 'scenery' in the windows. *British Rail.*

taken out and dusted down. In the summer of 1932 first the LNER, then the LMS and GWR in quick succession began renewed trials of buffet cars, and this time there was no groundswell of public disapproval; the first world war and its aftermath had radically changed social attitudes along with everything else.

Some of these first buffets were converted restaurant cars, but their success soon prompted the construction of new, purpose-designed stock. These cars took advantage of the improved technology available, such as electric lighting, ventilation, and refrigeration. Their main interior feature was a long buffet counter, and the seating for about two dozen customers was, on the LMS cars for example, 'built up on chromium-plated tubular steel frames, the cushions, seat-backs and arm-rests being filled with Dunlopillo and covered with terra-cotta buffalo hide' – the very pinnacle of 1930s fashion! Another notable build came a few years later when in 1938 the Southern Railway built for its newly-electrified Bognor line their highly distinctive art-deco Bognor Buffets, with scalloped edges to bar and tables and on the decorative partitions along the sides.

Buffet cars now found work on a variety of routes. Some, as on the Southern Railway, were shorter-distance runs where there was not really time to down a full meal. At the other extreme were very long journeys, such as the central part of the famed 790-mile Aberdeen-Penzance through service (operated by an LNER car), where leisure travellers welcomed the diversion of light refreshments on their great trek. Then there were 'specials,' such as the LNER 'Buffet Tourist Trains' serving the industrial North, where the Depression was biting hardest. These trains would be based at a series of centres for several days at a time, often tied in with the local Wakes Weeks, and running an excursion to a different destination each day. They offered the hard-pressed working folk a cheap and varied holiday without leaving home. Each train included a brake van fitted up with hammock hooks where each night the buffet staff slung their hammocks Navy-style, for like a road show they travelled around the country with the sets, moving overnight from one town to another.

As well as providing a new way to eat, buffet cars also recalled the pleasures of drinking. Thirty years before this had been their downfall, but now in a much-changed society it was a positive

Sophisticated drinking in the cocktail bar of the Coronation Scot, 1937. *British Rail.*

A typical junction station dining room of the inter-war years — adequate but uninspired. This is Newton Abbot in 1927. *BR/OPC.*

asset. We saw in a previous chapter how the licensing laws for many years made station refreshment rooms a tippler's paradise. On the trains, the possibilities were different. Each individual catering vehicle was deemed to require its own licence with an appropriate fee, for many years one guinea (£1.05), payable annually to Excise. This license held good only in the vehicle itself, so corridor trolleys, for example, had to be 'dry.' While the train was on the move drink could be sold at any hour, but when standing at a station the crew was supposed to adhere to the local licensing hours of wherever the train happened to be. This was clearly ridiculous, especially as licensing hours varied considerably between areas! Occasionally a local authority, motivated by some personal or political feud, would prosecute a railway for serving drink out of hours, but the sensible and generally-observed rule was not to open the bar before the train began its journey, and to close by arrival at destination. It was not until 1964 that the Licensing Act of that year granted full exemption from the licensing laws to railway passenger

vehicles, provided that a food service was also available.

One service which made the most of the possibilities was that between Cambridge and London, King's Cross. Introduced in the mid-1930s as the 'Garden Cities and Cambridge Buffet Expresses,' these short, smartly-timed trains were quickly nicknamed the 'beer trains' by the undergraduates from down the line. History has rather left the denizens of Welwyn Garden City and Letchworth where the trains called outside this hall of fame, but they too enjoyed a London service unique among satellite towns for its speed and liquid attractions.

In 1934 the Great Western Railway took buffets a stage further by building its first two Quick Lunch cars. These impressive vehicles had no orthodox seating at all, but in the words of the *GWR Magazine* their main feature was:

'a counter which extends for the whole length of the cars between small vestibules at each end which form the pantry and the wine cupboard, respectively. Twelve stand-up rest seats of the most modern design are arranged along the centre of the counter . . . a stainless steel foot-rail extends for the whole length of the counter, and accommodation is provided for hats, handbags etc, by means of a recess under the counter top.'

These cars, with their daring overtones of transatlantic informality, were pointing a direction yet to be taken on *terra firma* by Britain's railways.

The pleasures of the buffet car even spread to such unlikely byways as the narrow-gauge Welsh Highland Railway. For the last three years of its operation, from 1934 to 1936, this line ran a buffet service between Beddgelert and Dinas, and its ministrations must have been very welcome on a journey which, while advertised as a tourist highlight, was in practice all too often uncomfortable, rain-sodden, and very slow. The Welsh Highland also led the narrow gauge field by owning four small station refreshment rooms, managed for it by the Snowdon Mountain Hotels & Tramroad Co. With two refreshment rooms and three hotels of its own (Chapter 4), the Snowdon Mountain company must for a time have had a higher proportion of catering to railway interests of any British railway company!

Nationally, the refreshment room scene, which we left at the end of Chapter 3, had drifted into a long fallow period of little development – a similar situation, be it said, to the rather

The Swinging 'Thirties: new-style eating at the GWR Quick Lunch & Snack Bar, Paddington, May 1936. *Travellers Fare.*

lacklustre cafes typical of Britain's High Streets in those times. Little was done to redress matters for nigh on two decades, when the Great Western, becoming alarmed by the steady fall in receipts, began to make moves to brighten this tarnished image. Having broken new ground on trains with its Quick Lunch car, the GWR now followed this with a Quick Lunch bar at Paddington station. This modish eating-house, with its central servery and its counter round which travellers sat on high stools, enjoyed the same slightly raffish style of its railborne counterpart.

Elsewhere, the LMS had the biggest chain of refreshment rooms, each with its familiar 'Cup & Corkscrew' emblem outside the door, but these too had drifted far from the excellence of William Towle's day, so at the rebuilding of Leeds Wellington (later City) station in 1938, a milk bar was introduced to cater for the latest in public taste. This bar was separated from the main waiting room only by a glass screen with wide double doors, thus usefully advertising itself to passengers who might otherwise have gone unrefreshed.

This was the state of things when for the second time in a quarter-century, the darkness of total war descended across the land. Hostilities were declared on 3 September 1939, and this time there was to be no attempt to retain normal service. The railways again were placed under the control of a National Railway Executive Committee (working from offices at the disused Down Street station on London Underground's Piccadilly Line), and on Monday 11 September all restaurant car services were withdrawn. The main reason was the drafting of men into the armed forces, but there were others too: restaurant cars added extra weight to trains, while taking up valuable passenger space; some were needed for Red Cross and other war service trains; and not least, it rapidly became impossible for passengers to reach them through corridors stacked with luggage and soldiers' kit.

However, during the false calm of the 'phoney war' late in 1939 a few restaurant car services were re-instated, and these gradually increased in number. The official booklet *British Railways in Peace and War*, published in 1944, states that at the

Wartime emergency: in November 1940 the buffet at St Pancras in London hosted a temporary ticket counter when bombs severely damaged the official booking office. *Travellers Fare*.

end of 1941 'only' 426 services were running daily – a surprisingly substantial total. By May 1942 these had dwindled to 65, and from April 1944, with the D-day preparations, these too disappeared.

Virtually the whole burden of feeding the nation's railway travellers thus fell on the refreshment rooms – that under-invested and under-managed Cinderella among railway departments. Worse, some of the rooms were also closed, yielding up vital manpower or station space to more essential uses: 767 rooms were open at the outbreak of war, but this was down to 595 by 1944. So with most platform trolley services also withdrawn, refreshment rooms were perpetually crowded and short of supplies, conditions, no doubt, which prompted a wistful correspondent to write to *The Railway Gazette* in 1943:

> In days so different from these
>   They called you to the eating-car
> With 'Take your seats for luncheon, please!'
>   But now you line up at the bar
> For snacks and kickshaws in variety,
>   And drinks that don't affect sobriety.
>
> You pick and choose, and stand and eat,
>   Or take your portion to the train,
> And hope you'll find a corner seat,
>   And hope some day to hear again
> The luncheon call, and reach your table
>   And eat as much as you are able.

Kickshaws? A word that seems to have gone out with wireless sets and roast mutton, but for generations it meant something unsubstantial, trifling, or fancy.

While the railways struggled with their enormous load, the Luftwaffe was busy overhead. Most of the London stations suffered bomb damage to some extent, as did many others, and great quantities of catering equipment were lost. Among the most spectacular damage was the complete destruction of London's Holborn Viaduct, London Bridge, and Cannon Street Hotels, all of which had been converted to offices some years previously. At St Pancras the refreshment rooms doubled as a booking office when that was blitzed in May 1941, while King's Cross had a bomb smack through the roof of the dining room – empty at the time – which exploded in the restaurant car stores in the basement, causing considerable mayhem. To this day, an

Restaurant car services re-started on 1 October 1945, and chief steward Harry Wylie accepted bookings on the Flying Scotsman at King's Cross. *British Rail.*

observer across the road can see the great patched-up gap in the station building there.

The War was won by May 1945, but the effort left the nation's resources winded and struggling, and there set in a period of shortages and austerity that in some ways was worse than the war itself. With the challenge of danger over and victory achieved, the country faced the long uphill struggle of rebuilding against a backcloth of material drabness and erosion of old social standards. Meanwhile, the international situation remained tense with new uncertainties, and large numbers of men in uniform moved about the country.

Petrol rationing continued to throw extra loads upon the railways, and with accommodation on trains at a premium, restaurant car operations did not begin again until 1 October 1945; at first very limited, the service gradually grew as men and materials became available once more. Foodstuffs and hardware alike were in very short supply; no restaurant or café could serve meals of more than three courses, and customers were allowed a slice of bread *or* potato (very probably potato substitute) with their dinner, but not both. At the refreshment rooms, self-service was now increasingly the fashion. Every item of equipment was precious, and travellers not infrequently found the sole station teaspoon tied to the counter rail with string, a precaution against the depredations of acquisitive servicemen and others.

The general misery reach new depths when the terrible winter of 1947 engulfed the country. Fuel as well as food was desperately short, and all Britain shivered as the greatest blizzards in living memory brought normal life to a standstill. Trains became snowbound on the northern hills, some for several days, and dining car crews worked wonders keeping stranded passengers supplied with something hot, struggling desperately the while to eke out gas supplies.

Hope for the future in this delightful GWR menu for New Year's Eve 1945, its 'train' including the Great Western Royal Hotel at Paddington. But it was to be a full decade before things were back to normal. *Author's collection.*

A Happy New Year to our Patrons

DINNER MENU

Cream of Vegetables

Roast Pheasant & Chips
Brussels Sprouts   Parsnips Julienne
Potatoes

Christmas Pudding   Ice Cream
3/6 PLUS SERVICE CHARGE

ON THE "RAIL" TO GREATER ACHIEVEMENTS!

December 31st, 1945.

After the war the LNER took the lead in modernising its refreshment rooms. This is King's Cross (Suburban side) in late 1947. *Travellers Fare.*

Refreshment room services, not for the first time, found themselves facing the humdrum hardship without the excitement. Even when fame came their way, it did not flatter. Just such an instance now arose, which quite unintentionally was to shape images for years to come. In a screen version of Noel Coward's famous *Brief Encounter*, film stars Celia Johnson and Trevor Howard acted out their heartache in the station buffet at Carnforth, masquerading under the name of Ketchworth. Redolent of the restriction and drabness of those monochrome days, this film set is now something of a period 'collector's item', but for a couple of decades it seemed to present a mould from which railway buffets, like Noel Coward's luckless lovers, were unable to escape.

But amid the gloom, a new glimmer of light now appeared on the London & North Eastern Railway. This company's refreshment room supervisors traditionally reported to their area general management, not to any central catering control, and the management now decided that both the organisation and the rooms themselves were much in need of change.

The upshot was the creation of a new post of superintendent of refreshment rooms, who reported direct to the chief general manager, and the person brought in to fill this post was a most able and energetic manager by the name of E. K. Portman-Dixon. 'P-D', as he was universally known, had a very low base from which to start. Besides the shortages and run-down equipment there was a suspicion, not totally founded on fiction, that the qualifications for the post of refreshment room manageress included an ample girth, untidy hair and dirty overall, with the voice to bellow 'No cups outside!' in stentorian tones should any customer dare sidle, crock in hand, towards the door. In the face of all this, 'P-D' quickly embarked on a major refurbishment programme, starting in 1947 with Liverpool Street where labour-saving, easy-to-clean plastic panelling was installed. Even better, the company printed a special booklet instructing staff in how to make a good cup of tea!

Another far-reaching move was taking place on the Southern Railway, which in 1946 decided that better control would be exercised and value offered if it took over the management of its hotels and catering itself. The railway thus began setting up an in-house catering organisation, under a former Army catering chief with the highly appropriate name of Belcher, and plans were made to terminate the various private contracts as they came up for renewal. The new order had scarcely begun, however, when the Southern, along with all the other major railways in Britain, was once again overtaken by great events. This time those events were (in theory at least) the wish of the British people, but they were to bring with them trials and tribulations as far-reaching in their own way as those of the war so lately won.

7
Politics and Power

Just 2½ years after victory in Europe the railways of Britain, under a Labour Government elected by a landslide majority, were overtaken by the cataclysm of Nationalisation. This is not the place to argue political rights and wrongs, but from the point of view of getting things right for the customer there is no question that in those already difficult days the very last thing the railways and their catering needed was the turmoils and trials of a mammoth reorganisation. Worse, this particular upheaval was predestined to be unpopular with many of the railways' customers, for reasons totally unconnected with the railway *per se*.

The acts of Nationalisation stand of course at the very core of the country's party political warfare, so any public industry attracts automatic odium from certain sections of society, whether it is doing a good job or not. But there is another dimension. The same John Bull spirit which has kept the shores of Britain free of invaders for nine centuries, causes her people to view with suspicion and hostility any attempt by 'them' to impinge on daily life – an attitude by no means confined to one political party. Under Nationalisation, the railway ticket barrier and buffet counter began to look suspiciously like extensions of that popular enemy, the Whitehall desk. And if lumbered with Whitehall willy-nilly, John Bull's reaction is to ridicule and knock it.

This 'spirit of the free' manifests itself also in the British aversion to taking jobs in 'service.' Reinforced by the country's pervasive class structure, able people from the middle classes, unlike their continental counterparts, have often shunned careers such as catering where they might be called upon to defer to people no better than themselves. Consequently, catering management and catering staff have not always attracted their fair share of able, intelligent and personable recruits. Railway catering therefore now stood at both a political and a social disadvantage, and the old prejudices of Dickens' time, never very far down the comedian's joke list, now surfaced again with fresh topicality.

The first essential in tackling all this was a management and organisation devoted from the very top down full-time to the business. Unfortunately, that was just what the Transport Act of 1947 did not provide. Indeed, fully 34 years were to pass before this prime need was met, but like so many things it did not look so obvious at the time.

The Transport Act, which came into effect on 1 January 1948, was concerned among other things to concentrate the minds of railway managers on running railways. Hitherto, catering and hotels had (except on the Southern) been managed very much as railway functions, along with other activities such as steamers and docks, and an influential body of opinion held that this wide range seriously weakened the effectiveness of railway management. The new Act therefore established an overall governing body in the form of the British Transport Commission. To this Commission there reported various Executives, each charged with running one part of the transport industry – railways, road transport, docks, canals, London Transport, and not least the Hotels Executive, which included catering. Amid this massive reorganisation it was perhaps inevitable that railway catering and railway hotels should remain grouped together; their growing differences were but a trifle in this great new context.

This now meant that the Executive concentrated, as its named implied, on running the hotels first, with railway catering problems coming second in every way. The set-up of the organisation encouraged this; at its head (designated Chief Member) came F. G. Hole, a hotels man through and through, with four Area Hotel Superintendents under him; Headquarters departments such as Personnel were very much geared to Hotel staff business, and railway catering found itself represented at Headquarters only by two Superintendents, one for restaurant cars and one for refreshment rooms.

The Hotels Executive was charged like the other Executives with standing on its own feet financially and paying its way, taking one year with another. It was facing a formidable task. The year 1949, for example, was to show the hotels losing a total of £47,000, and though the refreshment rooms pulled in a £327,000 surplus the restaurant cars more than sank all this in a £514,000 deficit. (These figures mean rather more to today's reader when multiplied by 12 to bring them up to 1986 prices). The refreshment room profit, furthermore, was on a downward trend, with massive investment urgently needed to arrest it; the dining cars were still patently rooted in their traditional philosophy of providing a service regardless of cost. Indeed, one old catering manager of the author's acquaintance had been soundly rebuked by his LNER Hotels Superintendent not very long before World War II because a particular group of cars had shown a profit the previous year. His duty, he was reminded, was to cater for the railway's passengers, not to make a profit out of them!

In the new and straitened order it was perhaps understandable, if questionable, that the Executive devoted most of its resources to where the profits could most quickly be found. That meant a continuing emphasis on the better of the hotels, while many of the others, along with several refreshment rooms, were closed or sold. The restaurant cars, needed by the railways as a passenger service but financially embarassing to the Hotels Executive controlling them, now became a major bone of contention.

The Chairman of the Executive appointed to run this diverse range of assets was Lord Inman of Knaresborough, a man who came to the job with a reputation for success in the world of hospital fund-raising behind him. Lord Inman quickly earned respect for his sincerity, honesty and approachability. The Chairman's job in those pioneering days involved a great deal of symbolic and public relations work, and on the sticky wicket of the times he made a determined and praiseworthy effort to open the innings. It cannot have been an easy task, particularly when his partner at the crease was a personality as strong as the chief member, F. G. Hole.

Frank Hole, trained as an accountant with the LMS, had risen to be Controller of LMS Hotels before taking up his new post. Prominent on various committees in Britain's hotel and tourist industry, he devoted most of his time to the world he knew and understood, seldom intervening in the business of railway catering. A concerned and agreeable man, Hole was nevertheless held in awe by his staff for the tremendous hours he

E. K. Portman-Dixon, refreshment room supremo for British Railways from 1948, and later in charge of all railway catering. *Author's collection.*

worked, the range of his abilities, and not least for the volume of important paperwork which always filled his desk! This characteristic, caused no doubt by his accountant's training, was to prove the despair of his subordinates, for it meant that decisions on quite ordinary matters were often a very long time in coming.

With a lack of experience in popular catering at the top of the business, it was indeed fortunate that the superintendent of refreshment rooms was a person well able to direct operations without any need to look upward for guidance. E. K. Portman Dixon – 'P-D' from the LNER – had a background in contract catering management before joining the railways, and since the war had impressed everyone by his energy in reorganising and transforming his company's motley ragbag of station buffets – the worst, some said, of any of the Big Four companies. 'P-D' now set about the even more daunting task of bringing together and modernising the refreshment rooms nationwide.

On the very first day, as each manager received a dossier of questionnaires and instructions, it was obvious that life under this human tornado was changing dramatically. Recruiting his own teams and setting an example of thoroughly hard graft

A 1951 shot of the Platform 1 self-service buffet at Paddington – a scene epitomising the drabness of life in those post-war years. *Travellers Fare*.

himself, he inspired others to heights hitherto unknown, and it was not long before, despite all the troubles of rationing and shortages, 'P-D's momentum began to show through in rising profits and better service at the counter. If just one idea paid off out of several, ran his philosophy, then the time spent on them all was worthwhile. One such idea was the self-service cafeteria which had emerged from the labour shortage of the war. These places, with their much-reduced costs, now began to appear all over the system, while the station dining room with its table service of pinnied waitresses began the long road to ultimate extinction.

(*Opposite*)
Fish and game feature heavily in this 'austerity' menu for Broad Street dining room in 1949, when the retail price index was about one-twelfth its value for 1986. Despite the shortages, there is commendable variety – but note the restrictions on courses! *Author's collection*.

MENU

Iced Grape Fruit Cocktail, 9d.

Iced Sugar Melon & Ground Ginger, 1/-

Hors d'Oeuvres Variés, 3/3

Mock Turtle 6d.   Scotch Broth, 6d.

Omelettes:- Spinach, Cheese, Tomato, Spanish, 3/3

Fresh Eggs   Chicken or Mushroom, 3/6

B   Spaghetti Napolitaine or Bolognaise, 3/

B   Oeuf au Plat, Diana, 3/6

B   Curried Eggs Bouquetière, 3/6

B   Poached Egg, Florentine, 3/6

A   Egg, Stuffed Tomato, Mushroom & Bacon, 3/6

Fried Fillet of Plaice au Citron, 3/3

Fried Fillet of Sole, Sauce Tartare, 3/3

Fried, Grilled or Boiled Turbot, Hollandaise Sce. 3/3

Fried Scollops, Tomato Sauce, 3/3

Rainbow Trout, Vert Pré, 3/3

Red Mullet, Bordelaise, 3/3

Fried Fillet of Fresh Haddock, Tomato Sauce, 3/3

A   Steak, Chicken & Mushroom Pdg. or Pie, 3/3

A   Mixed Grill, 3/3

A   Curried Chicken, Maharaja, 3/3

A   Jugged Scotch Hare, Red Currant Jelly, 3/3

A   Lancashire Hot Pot & Pickled Cabbage, 3/3

A   Boiled Chicken, Parsnips & Parsley Sauce, 3/3

A   Braised Duckling aux Navets, 3/3

POULTRY BELOW SERVED HOT OR COLD

A   Roast Norfolk Turkey, Chestnut Stuffing, 3/3

A   Roast Goose, Sage & Onion, Apple Sauce, 3/3

A   Roast Duckling, Sage & Onion, Apple Sauce, 3/3

A   Roast Stuffed Chicken, Bread Sauce, 3/3

A   Roast Partridge sur Canapé, Game Chips, 3/3

A   Roast Pheasant sur Canapé, Game Chips, 3/3

A   Cold Steak, Chicken & Mushroom Pie, 3/3

Tomato, Green, Potato, Cress or Japonnaise Salad, 1/-

Mashed, Boiled or Baked Jacket Potatoes, 4d.

Braised Celery, 8d.   Greens, 6d.   Braised Onions, 8d.

Brussels Sprouts, 8d.   Cauliflower au Gratin, 8d.

Cauliflower, Cream Sauce, 8d.   Spinach, 8d.

Fresh Garden Peas, 8d.

Steamed Marmalade Pudding, 9d.

Blackberry & Apple Pie, 9d.   Baked Jam Roll, 9d.

Fresh Apricot Condé, 9d.   Gâteau Montpanasse, 9d.

Creamed Rice Pudding & Victoria Plums, 9d.

Ices:-   Vanilla or Chocolate, 9d.

Anchovies on Toast, 9d.

Mushrooms on Toast, 9d.   Welsh Rarebit, 9d.

Dessert:- Fresh Peach or Apricots, 1/- Tangerine 8d,

FOR WINE LIST SEE OVERLEAF

DINING ROOM   19/1/49.   **BROAD ST. STATION**

The superintendent of restaurant cars was a horse of a rather different colour. W. P. Keith had served under Hole on the LMS, and then moved to hotels superintendent on the GWR – a rather different department, if only because the Great Western had very few hotels. Willie Keith was the embodiment of that overworked phrase, 'one of nature's gentlemen.' An extremely popular chief, he operated the typical hotelier's policy of 'Not a ripple on the water.' This policy had been the watchword of the hotels in their golden days, but the restaurant cars were an altogether more rumbustious scene, and the business world in general was becoming a harder place. Keith found that the ripples on the water, far from being stilled, were threatening to turn into a tidal wave.

Already beset by political and economic troubles, the restaurant cars found themselves particularly badly hit by rationing and shortages. While refreshment room customers were generally looking for a snack, those in the restaurant cars expected something better – more what a hotel might produce.

Wartime neglect left a vast backlog of rooms that were dingy and uninviting outside as well as in. This is Glasgow Queen Street in June 1949. *Travellers Fare.*

Hotels were having problems enough in making the best of leftovers and cheap unpromising cuts of meat. Restaurant cars with their minuscule storage space and their ever-changing levels of demand faced a challenge indeed in conjuring up an appetising menu.

But dining car crews, ever an enterprising bunch, soon learned to make the most of whatever was available. At first sight this was precious little. The caterers' meat allowance, fixed by the Ministry of Food, stood at two-thirds of one-pennyworth (old pennies of course) of meat per meal served, based on a meal count taken over the previous month. With this meagre ration, customers could have potato or a slice of bread – but not both. Great volumes of paperwork, detailing precisely what had been consumed, had regularly to be sent up to the Ministry.

Certain basic foodstuffs escaped the Government's dictum, and notable among these were fish and game. The fish to be had was often whalemeat or the dreaded *snoek*, while into the category of game came pigeons, rabbits and goodness knows

what. A memorable feature of those days was the railways' Game Pie prepared in the hotels and also served (after a quick re-heat on board) in the restaurant cars. The game, said the staff, was to guess what was in it. A good chef could in fact make a very presentable dish out of this, but the smell that billowed down the corridor as the pastry crust was lifted was said to be often mighty strong!

The private citizen, less severely rationed, did not always understand the caterers' problems. Some, fed-up with the dreariness and austerity of life, decided that the shortcomings were all the Government's fault and, the railways being nationalised, took it out on the restaurant cars. As the war receded but shortages persisted, tempers got worse. Thus a writer in the *Glasgow Herald* in August 1948 complained:

> 'On a recent journey from Stirling to London, we were all rationed at lunch to a meagre portion of potatoes. At dinner there was none, only a few slices of bread; the chief attendant protested he was supplied by Headquarters in London with food for the 1,000 mile return journey. If it did not last, that was just too bad.
>
> 'That the crew of a dining car have no power to buy a couple of stones of potatoes to tide over an obviously approaching emergency is a dreary instance of the workings of centralised control. But it is also an illustration of how incompetently a big business is being run on behalf of the rest of us, who own the undertaking – theoretically. In the days of the old Caley and L&NW, somebody would have been sacked for these crass failures in simple matters. Organised Socialism has still to face the problem of discipline.'

Political bias apart, press cuttings of the period tell a largely unrelieved story of a fight against heavy odds. A steward interviewed in the *North-Eastern Weekly News* in July 1950 remarked sadly, 'I start by going round with aperitifs, but there's not much demand for them, these days.' It was the same further down the market. A headmaster in Oldham demanded to know why on his school's outing to London the catering department had substituted cold fried fish, jam tarts and biscuits for the ham and tongue sandwich, roll and butter, and fruit and jelly he had ordered. 'Many of the children threw the fish onto the railway line,' he observed drily, 'and there were complaints that the smell of the fish had penetrated the jam tarts.'

There was a feeling, too, that somebody else was always doing that bit better. 'According to the Hotels Executive of British

Railways,' said a writer on the London *Evening Standard*:

'the offer is frequently made of chicken, goose, salmon and trout, boiled beef, roast mutton, and steak and kidney pie.

'That this is undoubtedly true will be vouched for by the scores of thousands who have been told by train-waiters that these items are no longer available. It is amazing how often the lucky and anonymous passengers on the previous journey, or at the last sitting, have rifled the larder of its best comestibles and left oneself to choose among sausages, boiled cod, the infinite and illegitimate spawn of the spam family, semolina pudding, mashed swedes, and that special railway atrocity they call savoury rissole'.

The *Yorkshire Post* in April 1949 sent one of its writers on a fact-finding tour of trains and refreshment rooms in the North of England. His own opinion – and this in a newspaper not generally noted for its support of things Socialist – was that passengers were 'likely to be pleasantly surprised by dining-car fare' of the day, and 'would probably agree that it is better than that provided at most of the restaurants at home.' But there were plenty of grumbling customers around; as a steward said, 'They seem to think there's no such thing as rationing on trains.'

The station fare did not do so well, the food at York being in the reporter's words, 'just as dim and dingy as the rooms in which it was served. I was offered a haslet sandwich at one of them ("some kind of brawn, Sir. Never touch it myself") and a sausage-meat sandwich at the other ("some people call it haslet, Sir. I think it's a kind of haggis").' At Leeds, at the end of the day, the refreshment room was full of smoke and gloom and selling only some gargantuan teacakes lurking beneath glass covers. The intrepid reporter purchased one and peered inside. The contents 'peered back from the corners, dark and sinister in the half-light. It was haslet again!'

Lord Inman, Chairman of the Hotels Executive, was moved to explain some of the facts of dining car life in the *News Chronicle*, also in April 1949. The standard meal on trains, he declared, cost 4s 0d (20p). Of this, 2s 0d (10p) was taken in wages, 3½d (2p) in repairs and maintenance, 3d (2p) in fuel and light, and another 3d went on laundry and cleaning. That left 1s 2½d (6p) for food; but if, for example, the menu were sausage and cod, those items would actually cost 1s 8d (8p). That left a loss of 5½d (2½p) per meal, and the only redeeming factor was a profit of 8d (3p) made on drinks. He added that restaurant cars currently ran on 483

New counter displays, plus a return of branded goods, were beginning to lift the refreshment room image when this classic shot of Crewe was taken about 1952. *Travellers Fare.*

trains daily, shortly to rise to 588 with the summer timetable; and about 10 million meals a year were served in them.

This total of meals may sound impressive, as indeed it was, but changes in the social and travel scene were quickening, and train passengers were beginning to look for a less formal style of eating, as was happening in E. K. Portman-Dixon's refreshment rooms. Attention now turned to the Southern Railway, which with its shorter distances had been in the lead in buffet development before the war. One of the ideas the Southern had tried was the service of draught beer on board. This had not been an unqualified success, but the drinking theme seemed worth exploiting and in 1949 there appeared the series of well-known Tavern Cars.

One-half of the exterior of these remarkable vehicles was painted to resemble brickwork on the lower panels, with mock timbering above. Inside, the layout was based on the traditional pub, complete with bar, veneer woodwork and panelling, but the windows were confined to long narrow lights, just below the roof; passengers, unless they were over 6ft tall, could barely see out. As one of the chief pastimes on a train is looking out of the window, this feature proved most unpopular.

The decor outside was completed by painted inn-signs: *The Dolphin, White Horse, Jolly Tar, Salutation, Crown, Three Plovers, Bull,* and *Green Man.* It was a game attempt to bring a little interest and imagination to railway journeys, but the rather bizarre exteriors were too gimmicky for many people's taste, and the window problem alienated the very customers on whose goodwill success depended. There were letters to *The Times*, and the matter was raised in the House of Commons by Tom Driberg, MP. Despite a vigorous defence by a young Parliamentary Secretary by the name of James Callaghan, the tavern cars were soon retired from the scene.

As the 1940s ended, the country became more than ever determined to slough off the days of austerity and demonstrate to the world that John Bull had not lost his sense of fun and ceremony. Thus was born the Festival of Britain 1951, marking the Centenary of the Great Exhibition of Victorian times. In retrospect, the attempt at celebration was possibly premature; rationing was by no means over, and a change in the mood of the nation cannot easily be engineered or hurried. It was in fact to be the Coronation of Queen Elizabeth II, two years later, which quite dramatically *did* change the colour of life, ending the days of dreariness and marking the start of two decades of growth and prosperity.

The 'Jolly Tar', one of the remarkable Tavern Cars introduced on the Southern Region in 1949. Note the Atlantic Coast Express roof board, in this view taken at London Waterloo. *Crown Copyright. National Railway Museum, York.*

But the Festival of Britain involved everyone, British Railways included, in a major effort to brighten up their house and try out new ideas. A series of new rolling stock was built, incorporating restaurant cars and unclassed dining saloons, and intended for the prestige expresses of each railway region. Sadly, these restaurant cars were forced to use some anthracite-fired cooking equipment that had lain on hand since before the war – something we shall come to in the next chapter – and they led a brief and unpopular life. On the stations, the Festival logo appeared in redecorated buffets, along with decorative menu cards, though in truth there was usually little decorative about the menu contents.

It was in the following year that the first prototype cafeteria car came into service. Converted from an ex-LNER vehicle, it offered a service of light takeaway meals, and was economical on staffing, with customers helping themselves on a tray and paying the cashier at the end of the counter. This system was something entirely new for railway vehicles; trains in those days rode rather less smoothly than they do today, and customers found themselves having to learn the stewards' art of carrying without spilling – not something that comes without a little practice.

Cafeteria cars featured in a variety of trains, but they met their greatest success in the 'cheap and cheerful' market, notably the Starlight Specials which operated well into the 1960s. These services, running through the night between London and Scotland, made use of trains and track that would otherwise be under-employed; made up of seating vehicles (not sleepers), they ran at parcels train speeds (to fit in with other night time traffic), between stations and over routes little used by daytime expresses. The simple, one-plate meals could be pre-prepared in the refreshment rooms at either end of the journey, and the staff were volunteers from various railway departments and offices, earning some very useful overtime. To load and unload these trains, the refreshment rooms staff at Marylebone station in London, for example, would be on duty until 1.00 am on summer weekends, the morning shift starting again just four hours later.

This move towards 'popular' catering was just getting into its stride when British Railways was faced with its second massive management shake-up in the space of five years. The British

A passenger lights eagerly upon her choice in the narrow confines of the first cafeteria car, 1952. *British Rail.*

Transport Commission, established in 1948, had proved unable to agree with its various Executives just where the responsibilities of the Commission ended and those of the Executives began. The trouble was greatest with the Railway Executive, for its senior management comprised traditional railwaymen who resented policy being dictated from bureaucratic heights, and, worse, interference (as they saw it) in the day-to-day running of their business.

The climax of the matter was the passing of the Transport Act of 1953, which abolished the various Executives altogether.

Their powers were now split between the Commission, whose strength was much reinforced, and new senior management levels in the railways and associated businesses. The Hotels Executive now became British Transport Hotels and Catering Services, headed by the Chief of Hotels and Catering Services, F. G. Hole. Second in command came the former restaurant cars manager, W. P. Keith, as Chief Hotels Officer and Assistant to the Chief of Hotels & Catering Services – a title surely worthy of a place in *The Mikado*. But next in line came the real power behind the railway catering throne, E. K. Portman-Dixon, now elevated to Chief of both Restaurant Cars and Refreshment Rooms.

The main purpose of this reorganisation was to solve a railway problem. With hindsight, it was another missed opportunity to separate the hotels and catering businesses, whose markets were diverging with increasing rapidity. Even so, Portman-Dixon, in charge of the entire railway catering scene, now wielded more power than the combined superintendents under the old regime, and for the first time also each railway Region had its own regional catering superintendent. It was the first step down what was to be a long road.

The old Hotels Executive, along with several other Executives, had had its headquarters at 222 Marylebone Road, NW1 – the former Great Central Hotel bought by the LNER in 1946 for conversion to offices. In its new guise, it now split itself into two. The Hotels HQ moved a couple of miles east, to another former railway hotel – the Midland Grand at St Pancras, closed in 1935 and taken over as offices by the LMS Hotels Division; the railway catering offices remained at Melbury Terrace, hard by Marylebone station, and it was to be fifteen years and two further moves before the two arms of the business were to meet again. Physical separation was proving rather easier than disentangling the strands of a business now more than a century old.

8
Life on the Cars

The special train was just fifteen minutes out of King's Cross when the cook, ready to start on the main course of lunch, called out to his assistant, 'Bring in that hamper of chickens, mate!' For a few moments there was just the noise of the train speeding over the track, and then, from the pantry next door, the rather nervous reply: 'There's no chickens here!'

The train, King's Cross to Leeds and back, first class only, had had special attention that day in 1938 from the LNER management. Morning coffee was already going round, and once through Peterborough, the crew would be at full stretch – 300 luncheons to serve, and 300 dinners on the way back. On board were the shareholders of a major company, visiting their main works in the North, but what was not on board, it now transpired, was the raw material for the next meal. Several dozen chickens, ready for the oven, were reposing instead on a barrow somewhere on King's Cross station.

The cook on a train can hardly send round to the local store when such misadventure happens, and the chances of obtaining enough birds at any intermediate stop would be slim indeed. But this particular train, like many specials, had no booked stops at all. There was nothing for it but face up to the senior company director on the train. To the intense relief of all this gentleman proved an affable soul, quickly agreeing to the dinner menu being brought forward to luncheon.

The immediate crisis over, there was now enough breathing space to organise a rescue. Word had to be got to King's Cross to locate the missing fowls and speed them on their way to Leeds. But in those days, there was no way of communicating with the 'shore', or with the driver (nor indeed is there on most trains, even today). So the chief steward now turned to the railway's traditional secret signalling system – writing a note and putting it inside the cut of a potato. As the train sped past stations and sidings, anxious pairs of eyes strained from the kitchen for sight of a railwayman at whom to lob this crucial projectile. But station after station seemed completely deserted, until somewhere near Huntingdon a lone signalman on the balcony of his little cabin spied a white-sleeved arm waving from the approaching special and, with a swish and a thud, a large potato crashed into the long grass just down the line. Faced with such a missile, a signalman could expect anything from sudden illness on the train – summon an ambulance to the next station – to a request for, well, chickens to be sent from King's Cross. Telegraph wires began to hum, and when the special reached Leeds and its well-lunched customers disembarked, up hurried the station dining car inspector. The potato had done its job, and King's Cross had been on the telephone to say that three dozen chickens were already well on their way.

Not every day brings such an embarrassing incident, but on the restaurant cars a crew is always out on its own, at the mercy of unforeseen hitches and delays, for up to 13 or 14 hours at a stretch. In that time its members will cook, serve and wash up for many hundreds of hungry and demanding travellers, not to mention the continuous coming and going at the buffet counter. Even today, nearly everything is freshly cooked on board – and cooked in a kitchen smaller than that of the average surburban three-bedroom house, which by contrast would seldom prepare meals for more than six people. A kitchen on a train incidentally is always a kitchen and never a galley, and its master is a cook, not a chef.

In a life like this, no crew member lasts the course for long without a sense of humour and an ability to get along with one's fellow human beings, while a good measure of initiative and resourcefulness is also very useful. Constantly out of step with the rest of the world because of their long and anti-social hours, cooks and stewards depend upon each other, yet are independent as a team, and not surprisingly consider themselves by tradition somewhat apart from other railway staff.

This notion of a breed apart has certain parallels with life on board ship, and it may have been no coincidence that James Bower, the conductor on that very first British dining car back in 1879, had run away to sea before fetching up with Pullman in Chicago. It attracts the same people – something particularly true in the age of the great ocean liners, when many older stewards, looking for less prolonged absences from home, took jobs on the dining cars for the latter years of their working lives. Women and girls have only recently entered the service in any numbers; in part this is a result of the changing status of women in society, though whether it also had anything to do with the heavy womanising for which sailors are known, is a matter for speculation!

The fascinating and half-hidden world behind the kitchen door has long possessed a certain mystique in the eyes of the railway passenger. The skills of its inhabitants demand respect; keeping one's 'sea legs' while carrying laden dishes on a swaying, lurching train is a knack that cannot be learned anywhere else. 'You mustn't resist the train, you must be flexible, and sway with it,' as a Newcastle steward explained to a journalist, 'and you mustn't look at the people you are serving, or you start to stagger – you've got to keep your eyes fixed in front of you when you're walking, and on what you're doing when you're serving. And if you've had a bad night, you couldn't do it at all.'

In the world of catering, notorious for its high turnover of labour, restaurant cars have the distinction of a turnover rate only about one-quarter of that on *terra firma*. The highly individual life runs in the blood, and jobs are even now handed down from father to son, harking back to the days when Dad would warn his youngest, proudly off on his first day as a pantry boy, that he might be sent to the driver to get a bucket of steam. Crews love the life for its challenge, its responsibility, and its variety. They are everything from maitre d'hotel to wine experts to washer-up. They are often the first line of information on a train. They are expected (though they seldom do!) to know all about train timetables and railway geography. They are nursemaids to babies, escorts to unaccompanied children, nurses to people taken ill, ambassadors for the railway, and mechanical geniuses if anything goes wrong with their equipment en route. They have to be; there is no hotel fitter to call on. And they are also nearest to hand if there is any blame about. But not infrequently gratitude is also the order of the day, even in the rush and pressure of the late twentieth century. Not so long ago, 70 hungry choristers had to be fed on the brief 50-minute journey between Plymouth and Exeter, and the chief steward and his crew worked flat out to serve the meals quickly.

The choristers were fed in time, and as the train approached Exeter they showed their appreciation: they stood and sang the staff a chorale.

On a long railway journey, drivers and guards can change over at intermediate points, but not so the restaurant car staff. For meal service, from preparation, through two or even three sittings, to the final washing-up and cashing-up, is a continuous job many hours long. Furthermore, preparation for the next meal will be going ahead while the present one is being served. All this calls for the exceptional hours of duty that are a hallmark of the job, and for very many years, lodging turns, involving one or more overnight stays, were commonplace. Even today some remain, whereas for enginemen and guards they are now firmly a thing of the past. The railway companies provided hostel accommodation for lodging in many main centres, but at peak times, particularly holidays, the men had to make do with very basic bed and board. The LNER tourist buffet trains of the 1930s described earlier, had the staff sleeping in hammocks strung up in the luggage van – shades of the Navy again – while the summer weekend traffic to the West Country between the wars saw crews spending Friday night on railway office floors at centres like Newton Abbot, or even in the cars themselves as they stood in sidings.

Though trains today are faster, rolling stock is used far more intensively and staff and cars now often do two return trips where they used to do one, calling for as much hard work as ever. One buffet car steward on the Euston-Wolverhampton run describes a day typical of the times when this line was electrified in the mid-1960s:

'Living in Edgware, I have to wake at 4.45am. By 6.15am I'm at Euston; officially I don't start till 6.45am, but getting there early means I get all my preparations done without too much rush. In this job, all you think of the whole time is getting your work done in time.

'Firstly I go to the linen room and get my uniform, and the table cloths, too. Then to the dry stores to pick up my stock and susts'. [Stock always means bar stocks in the traditional parlance of the trade, while 'susts' is short for sustentation – an old-fashioned world for foodstuffs that the dictionary defines as 'support of life'!] 'I've put an order in the night before for whatever I might need. Then I go to the cellar and pick up that order. A porter takes all this to the train, and we put it away, and lay the tables for breakfast, and make all the sandwiches.

Inside a Great Eastern Railway kitchen car, 1907. Note the array of gas taps, the guard rail keeping massive pans on the range, and piles of plates strapped onto the shelves. *British Rail.*

'The public don't realise how much background work there is in this job, nor how much paperwork I have to do. There are stock sheets, time sheets, takings sheets, summary sheets, plus a daily report – and much of this has to be fitted in during the journey, as well as the serving and strapping-up.' [Strapping-up means washing-up and putting-away – a relic of the days when piles of dishes were strapped onto shelves to stop them falling out]. 'People don't realise how pushed you are. We have to have our own breakfast in Wolverhampton sidings in the twenty minutes while the train is being cleaned.

'But I really *like* the job, and I like the public, and you never know just who you're going to meet or what they'll do. Only the other day there was this well-known MP who wanted to sit in a non-smoker, which wasn't laid up. I said he could, and I let him have kippers too, though they weren't on the menu. Afterwards I asked him for his autograph. He said: "I never put pen to paper. I seduce other men's wives, but I never put pen to paper", and swept out!'

The kitchen of this GWR car, photographed in 1914, appears very dark and gloomy. Note that the range is fitted *across* the vehicle, rather than along its length. *BR/OPC*.

Lecherous MPs apart, the constant pressures and the ever-present possibility of the unexpected have been familiar to every dining car steward since that first run in 1879.

Just as the staff have to be something of a special breed, so do the vehicles in which they work. Catering cars are at once a grocer's store, wine merchant's cellar, tobacconist, hotel kitchen, store-room and pantry. They must carry a refuse bin area, and there is wardrobe, locker and dressing space for up to eight staff, plus a toilet. Before World War II, when most of the business lay in full meals rather than buffet service, vehicles booked to do a return trip during the day might set off with supplies for as many as 500 full meals (unless there was a major depot at the far end). Also on board would be 1,250 plates, 250 teapots, cups and saucers, 250 coffee cups and saucers, 1,000 glasses, and 2,500 pieces of cutlery, as well as all the silverware, cruets, and jugs.

This was catering on the grand scale, and on a train it was ever a case of demanding a quart out of a pint pot. Early in the dining car saga, the staff began to develop ways of meeting these demands, and one of the most basic was the use of 'swing' service, where a kitchen car would be marshalled between two dining saloons. The crew would serve the first course to all the passengers in one saloon, and then 'swing' into the other, so that the first lot of passengers were always one or more courses ahead. This kept the staff together as a team, working at a constant rate, and the cook furthermore could spread main course service into two more manageable groups of 50 or 60 people each. The largest kitchen cars, those serving up to 240, had two complete kitchens with a full crew based in each.

'Swing' service today is seldom used except on heavily-loaded special trains, but another dining car tradition, dictated by lack of space, is still going strong. Silver service, where the food is served at table from silver dishes onto plates set before the customer, is sometimes considered old-fashioned and formal. Yet the simple truth is that the more modern plated service, with the basics of each course put onto plates in the kitchen, and then taken round to customers, demands considerable space for the plates to be spread out and filled. In restaurant cars there is no such space, so silver service reigns supreme.

Other tricks of the trade help to make a difficult job possible. A hotel waiter will probably serve the entire meal to each of his allotted tables, but on the trains, the shape and space of the cars demand that each steward in succession serve one particular item to everybody. To guide those about to serve, the one taking the orders may well play shorthand with the cutlery in front of the diner – a spoon placed diagonally means porridge ordered, a knife laid across the top indicates kippers, and so on. Many a tidy-minded passenger, not knowing the system, must have subconsciously moved the knives and spoons back when the order-taker had moved on, but memories are good and there is a back-up system on the back of a menu card, and not often are passengers left without their orders.

Whatever the dodges devised by the staff, there are no short cuts in designing and building the kitchen cars themselves. They must be exceptionally solid, to carry the weight of stoves, grills, refrigerators and sinks, plus all the stores. Such solid construction is an aid to another important quality, security, for with drink and tobacco aboard they are very vulnerable to burglary while standing in carriage sidings at night. Heavily-built vehicles usually ride solidly, which is as well because customers do not take kindly to vehicles which buck and jump at speed, causing soup and coffee to lunge alarmingly at them. Neither can the staff work when drenched by flying washing-up water. Washing-up sinks are therefore very deep and are never filled more than half-full, while the unseen water tanks in the vehicle are fitted with baffles inside, to prevent the dangerous surges which would otherwise take place with sudden stopping or starting of the train.

Water supply is one of the most important parts of a restaurant car, and over the years, when customers have been unable to get the advertised restaurant car service, the chances are high that something has gone wrong with the water system. A tremendous lot of water is needed; modern cars carry around 250 gallons, of which 50 gallons may be used on a long journey for tea and coffee alone. The rest must cover not only cooking but also the prodigious amount of washing-up involved, plus washing and cleaning of working surfaces, shelves and floors. Water supply can even today be touch-and-go on a long run, and where possible, crews wash salads and greens in the depots beforehand.

Restaurant cars built before Nationalisation generally had their water tanks fitted in the roof. The obvious advantage of this was that the water ran down to the taps inside by gravity, while in winter-time it had another priceless asset – the warm air in the vehicle rose to the roof and prevented the water from freezing. But it had its disadvantages also. Heavy water tanks at a height did not make for stability when under way. The fillers were on the rooftop and, if a lid did not fit tightly or was not properly fastened down, smoke and grime would quickly get in, lending a strange property to the tea and coffee being brewed below. Furthermore, the tanks were filled by a man climbing up onto the roof with a long hosepipe connected to a tap at ground level; when not in use, these hosepipes lay beside the track, and railway tracks are not the cleanest of places. Collars fitted round the hosepipe mouths went some way toward solving this problem but when overhead electrification began to come in, the

Watering the restaurant car with a trackside hose at Cardiff, June 1957. This former GWR 'Dreadnought' car was originally built as far back as 1904, and rebuilt in 1936. *D. Rouse.*

antics of men with hosepipes on roofs clearly had to end, so filling nozzles were fitted at buffer height, the water being forced up into the tanks (hopefully) by mains pressure.

Cleansing of these inaccessible tanks presented problems, and regular chlorination was essential. However, when vehicles began to come back into use after the long lay-off of World War II, many were in such a state that the water coming out of the tanks looked much like tea even before any tealeaves were put in. Overtime was quickly arranged, men got to work and public complaints were few, but the chief steward did wonder what was afoot one day when a lady customer asked him to bring her a soup plate full of cold water. Puzzled, the steward complied, whereupon the lady took a container from her bag and from it produced a small terrapin, which she placed in the water for a swim. All concerned completed their journey happily, but as the steward remarked, 'you just can't tell with the public . . .'

Soon after British Railways was formed in 1948, a new range of standard passenger rolling stock was commissioned, and against this background of diverse problems the catering vehicles were designed with their water tanks underslung between the frames. Construction of these cars continued up to 1962, and several of the later vehicles remain in service today. Increased stability was promised, and the greater accessibility of tanks would be valuable, especially in view of the much tighter hygiene regulations then coming into force.

The water in these cars was raised up to tap level by a small electric pump, but it was not very long before the staff found that these pumps were not entirely reliable. There was an emergency hand pump as well, but the entire system depended upon the filler caps being screwed back tightly after use, otherwise massive airlocks got into the system and rendered all the pumps useless. But the worst failing of the new cars was that the underslung tanks and pipes froze as soon as the weathermen sneezed. The full fleet of new cars was just about in service when the country was gripped by the Arctic winter of 1963, and frozen tanks now threw the catering into unprecedented chaos just when catering was most needed. Winters of this severity are rare, but the troubles have persisted intermittently ever since, sometimes to the fury and incomprehension of passengers who arrive at Euston on a seemingly mild day to find their restaurant car 'frozen up'. Weather conditions vary considerably on a long run. A journey down from Glasgow, when the weather is cold in Scotland, can be enough to put these vulnerable water systems out of action for several hours, for the speed of the train adds a wind chill factor to low temperatures. When the Mark III restaurant cars began to come off the production line in 1976, one and all were thankful to find the water tanks placed once more at roof level.

Just as important as the water supply is the cooking equipment. On the first Pullman restaurant cars, cooking was done on a coke stove, while the Midland Railway in the 1890s tried coal. The hazards of both these fuels in such a confined space were obvious, and about the turn of the century gas became standard for both cooking and lighting. Oil gas, with its highly distinctive smell which used to hang about old restaurant cars, still evokes memories for older travellers for it remained in use right up until the 1960s, particularly on London Midland metals. It was far more reliable than coal or coke, but it carried with it one grave disadvantage – the danger of fire in case of accident. This was horribly demonstrated on the Midland's Settle-Carlisle main line in 1910 and 1913, when at the two disasters of Hawes Junction and Ais Gill, within three years and three miles of each other, the wreckage was quickly turned into an inferno by the escaping oil gas, with heavy loss of life.

Although restaurant cars were not directly involved in either accident, the perils of this fuel were only too evident.

The Great Western Railway, individual as ever, used town gas, main carriage depots having the smelly job of regularly recharging the cylinders under restaurant cars. Smaller termini with no gas mains would instead replace empty cylinders with full ones, and gas cylinder wagons could be seen ferrying this equipment about the old GWR right up until the 1960s.

Electricity had by 1900 become a practical source of power on land, and after World War I Nigel Gresley, Chief Mechanical Engineer of the LNER, decided to harness its power for on-train cooking. He was faced with a major problem: cooking equipment uses a great deal of electricity, and on non-electrified lines, which in those days meant everywhere except the Southern, adequate supplies were not going to be easy.

While the train was travelling at speed, all was comparatively well. Dynamos beneath the floor driven by belts from the carriage axles fed the kitchen, and unless these belts were worn or slack power was adequate up to a point. But when travelling at less than about 15mph, or standing at a station, the dynamos delivered insufficient 'juice' and power had to be drawn from massive batteries, also slung beneath the frames. These batteries would be charged by the dynamos at speed but here was something else that had to be properly maintained, and if it was not a whole trainload of hungry diners could be let down.

Lengthy stands in stations or sidings, where considerable cooking might well be going on, demanded a much beefier power supply than batteries and the only answer was, quite literally, to plug into the mains. Gresley now installed massive electric sockets, with heavy lids, at major stations and sidings the length of the East Coast route. These 'pots', as they were known to the men, were spaced every couple of coach lengths or so, and when a train was at a stand it was the job of an electrician to connect the kitchen car with heavy lengths of cable rather like elephants' trunks, 2in thick and up to 65ft long. This meant employing a considerable number of extra electricians, adding more to the costs of an already expensive scheme.

The safety devices built into this system were ingenious. No electrician could obtain access to the plug-in point on a vehicle without pulling a lever which destroyed the vacuum brake in the train, thus preventing the driver from setting off with the restaurant car still plugged-in. A few minutes before the 'off' the electrician would shout a warning that the car was 'coming off the plug', and that was the signal for the cook to pull a large lever in his kitchen which changed the power source from mains to batteries and dynamos. This lever had a central 'neutral' position which had to be engaged when the kitchen was not in use – a particularly important precaution if the wooden duck-boards were for any reason taken up from the floor. If there were any electrical fault in the equipment, failure to do this could lead to the crew coming into contact with live surfaces, and at Leeds Central one day, while 'laying over' between trips, a cook's assistant neglected the instructions, took up the duckboards to clear some spillage, and paid the price with his life. It was the first and only fatality in the history of the LNER's electric cooking system.

While 'on the plug', a cook could use all his equipment, but once off it he was limited to a maximum of 60amp. That meant

'A Merry Christmas on the Flying Scotsman,' 1931. The vehicle is one of Gresley's electric kitchen cars, its array of switches and fuses controlling dynamo, batteries and mains supply. *BBC Hulton Picture Library.*

Christmastide between the wars brought the kitchen crews into the public limelight: the Royal Scot at Euston, 21 December 1936. *BBC Hulton Picture Library.*

perhaps one oven, one hotplate, one hot cupboard, one water urn and possibly one grill, and anything else would have to go off. If the cook turned over to batteries with too much kitchen equipment on, a safety switch blew; provided the train was at a standstill, he then turned off sufficient appliances and re-set the switch. If he overloaded the circuit while the train was under way another switch, known as the 'field' switch, blew, and this could not be re-set until speed had dropped below the crucial 15 mph. Meanwhile the current would be off altogether, so if this happened at the start of a long spell of fast running, and dinner was in the oven, the cook was in real trouble. It was such a situation that prompted one cook to try and out-wit the field switch by wedging it with a wooden spoon. There was a crack that threw him right across the kitchen, and several hundred pounds' worth of damage was done in a fraction of a second. Had he used a metal object, or his finger, he would certainly not have lived to tell the tale. After that, no-one else was ever known to try it.

This assortment of hazards did not help the smooth

preparation of meals, and though the system spread to the Great Eastern and Great Central lines of the LNER, it remained something of a liability on the East Coast main lines where business was much heavier. Because of the limitations imposed while under way, staff did as much pre-cooking as possible while 'on the plug.' The kitchens of the railway hotels were also brought into the scheme of things, notably those which enjoyed direct and convenient access to the station platforms, such as the North British in Edinburgh and the Great Eastern at Liverpool Street. Soups and sweets were pre-prepared in the depots as a matter of routine, and joints often had to be set-off (partly cooked) or even fully-cooked before being put on board. If skilfully done, setting-off can positively enhance a good joint, but the final re-heat in the oven is of course all-important, and cooks would aim to do this while 'on the plug.' If late running of the train seriously cut down this time, the odd customer, unaware of what was going on, may have found his meat a shade underdone.

There was thus great relief on the LNER when towards the end of the 1930s Doncaster Works turned out a series of anthracite-electric cars. The lighter equipment in these kitchens such as grills and coffee making machines were electric, but the ovens and ranges were heated by anthracite. The heat from an anthracite fire comes from hot gases, not flames, so the secret was to have a small white-hot fire, and an electric fan was fitted in the flue duct to generate a good draught. Anthracite is a clean fuel; with its various advantages, the LMS and the GWR experimented with it, as did British Railways with the 1951 Festival of Britain stock. Inexperienced crews were prone to put on far too much, killing the fire and blocking the ducts, and before the system could become really well established it was overtaken by another form of fuel, propane gas.

Propane, fitted in the new British Railways standard stock of the 1950s, was a significant advance over anything used previously, particularly on London Midland territory, for the LMS, despite the horrific accidents mentioned before, had persevered with oil gas fuel right up to Nationalisation. Propane gas demanded a new technique among crews. Unlike oil gas, it does not run along the burners when first lit, especially in cold weather, and many a cook who thought he had lit his oven unknowingly blew it out again by shutting the door too quickly after lighting-up from cold. Gas then built up in the oven and if a burner on the range was alight the next time the door was opened, there could be a minor explosion that banged the oven door hard back, giving the unfortunate cook a nasty crack on the knee. This did not have to happen more than once to most cooks!

Propane, still in use on a number of older vehicles, is more economical than oil gas, and it was found that two cylinders under each car sufficed, designated 'main' and 'reserve' on a little dial. As one cylinder became empty and the cook switched to 'reserve', a needle on the dial would indicate accordingly, and it was then the job of depot staff to change the empty cylinder and re-set the dial. Human fallibility being what it is, it was not unknown for sidings staff to re-set the dial while forgetting to change the cylinder. Next morning, in the middle of preparing breakfast for a hundred souls, the dreaded cry 'Out of gas!' and other things as well no doubt would be heard in the kitchen.

As electrification spread to the West Coast Main Line in the 1960s, another hybrid series of catering vehicles appeared in the form of the 1966 Manchester and Liverpool Pullman cars (Pullman by then being a division of British Transport Catering Services). Grills and water were heated by electricity supplied down the train by the locomotive, and drawn in turn from the overhead, but the ovens remained fuelled by propane gas. Not until the advent of the Inter City 125s in the mid-1970s did all-electric kitchens, with their microaire ovens (which cook simultaneously by convection and microwave), finally become standard.

Beside well-planned cooking facilities and water supply, restaurant cars demand good ventilation. This is not just a matter of the comfort of staff and passengers, though in the cramped conditions of the kitchen that is important enough. Condensation must be minimised or it will ruin the food, while the kitchen temperature must be kept down to a level where the refrigerators can cope properly. Modern vehicles have electric fans, but for many years the most sophisticated equipment available was a simple louvre in the roof. This primitive vent, one of the several pieces of gubbins that distinguished the roofline of old restaurant cars, could be moved from inside to face forward or backward, or be closed altogether. But if through poor maintenance it became stiff or jammed, there was nothing to stop billows of sulphurous train smoke cascading in, covering man and meat with a layer of sticky grime. A line particularly prone to this problem was the Great Northern section of the LNER, which has plenty of tunnels and whose steam coal from the mines around Doncaster gave off a peculiarly pungent smoke.

Adjusting the heating and ventilation for the comfort of passengers was very firmly the responsibility of the staff, and for years this was spelt out in the rule books with a typical Victorian authority. The Midland Railway *Regulations for Restaurant Car Staff*, dated 1920, include this directive: 'Stewards must . . . keep well in touch with the guards of the trains, and advise them when it is necessary for either more or less heat to be supplied, frequently looking at the thermometers.' Well-intentioned this may have been, but amid all the rush and pressure of meal service on board one imagines it was more honoured in the breach than in the observance.

The further back in time one goes, the more rigorous does life on the cars appear. In the days when employees were organised to assert their rights in the face of Victorian oppression, the trade union journal *Railway Review* was founded – a journal that lives on today in the guise of the National Union of Railwaymen's *Transport Review*. This publication traditionally carries views which might not in the way of things make the columns of more broadly-based prints, but it offers *per se* some glimpses of life deserving wider recognition. Thus a contribution to the *Review* of 30 March 1906:

'Sir, I was very glad to see . . . your fearless and open exposure of the locomen's treatment in the House of Commons, and I should like to mention a grade which is little heard of, and which is very hardly dealt with, *viz*, the saloon attendants. These men are paid a weekly salary, and it does not matter how many Sundays they are called upon to work – they get no remuneration whatsoever. Yet if they happen to be ill for even one day, their pay for the day is deducted from their wages. They are subject to fines and even dismissal for the most flimsy things conceivable, and if some of those fussy things called ladies and gentlemen happen to report these men it usually means instant dismissal.

'The long service and character of an attendant is never for one moment considered, but without a chance being given to defend his actions he is promptly paid off. A short time ago a cook and an attendant were both dismissed for not handing the sauce in a boat provided for the purpose, and . . . one of our directors, who takes an active part in temperance work among the employees, reported this case. These men were never given opportunity of defending their conduct, although they had reasons for acting in the manner they did.'

This letter, which goes on to bemoan the attendant's weekly rate of pay – 14s 2d (71p) – and that of the page boys – 9s 9d (49p) for a 70–80hr week – is signed darkly 'One in the know.' There are hints in this story that skulduggery may have been going on behind the scenes, and that management may have been seizing on an excuse to get rid of a ne'er-do-well employee. Even so, the precarious nature of a serving man's life and the whimsies of his master to which he was subject, remind one that for many the good old days were nothing more than a lifelong grind; on restaurant cars, with their added pressure and aggravation, life must have been more than usually uncomfortable.

Equally fearsome in those times were the autocratic chief restaurant car conductors, whose staff called them 'Sir' and who took little part in the service of meals, except to the especially favoured client. These men, seated in the saloon in solitary state after service had finished, had to be waited on before the crew members could sit down for their own meal. These chiefs asserted their authority in many ways, such as being very parsimonious in sharing out the tips, with the young boys, who worked hardest of all, getting the least. Crew members who failed to satisfy the chief got deductions from their share, and on appeal to the management they would be told that 'gratuities were not a matter in which the management intervened!'

Rigours like this were the lot of hotel staff everywhere, but restaurant car crews in addition faced a peculiar set of hazards, for trains, in moving about the country, are subject to sudden changes and uncertainties in ways that never befall a hotel or café. Major sporting events, notably horse racing, will double the number of meals served on certain lines even today, and the top meetings once demanded the running of several specials as well. On Grand National Day in 1911, for example, six specials left Euston for Aintree between 7.15am and 9.00am with ten cooks and twenty-four stewards *each*. A total of 3,500 meals was served, requiring (according the LNWR press handout) this massive inventory: 350 loaves, 6,000 rolls, 8,000 pats of butter, 5,000 eggs, 400 quart soup, 850 lb fish, 600 pr slips, 1,500 lb meat, 150 capons, 200 lb ham, 3,000 tartlets, 40lb tea, 70 lb coffee, 60 gall milk, 60 quart cream, 2,300 bottles of beer, 220 of whisky, 4,000 of mineral water, 1,000 cigars, dessert, etc. 'A goodly list indeed', observed the *Sporting Life* soberly, whereas the rival *Sporting Times*, the 'pink 'un', listing the same figures, commented: 'Wow, wow, wow! How do they *dooo* it?'

While events like the Grand National can be foreseen and planned for, others cannot, and these have not diminished with the years. Fog at airports can now mean a jumbo-load of passengers descending, for example, on Manchester Piccadilly Station, all bound for London, all demanding dinner, and all in a bad mood that does not improve when they learn that they will have to wait until the booked passengers have finished. Football fans play havoc with the best-laid plans, and trains may be declared 'dry' in advance to minimise the danger from drunken hooligans. Sir Francis Head's plea for temperance to the manageress at Wolverton Refreshment rooms has been answered, 130 years on – but the 'drought' is not to the liking of regular buffet customers!

Railway operating troubles and breakdowns are traditionally the bane of restaurant car men, who have no control over them but suffer considerable public kickbacks, and are landed with a great deal of extra hard work to boot. In all the history of railway catering there can have been no greater source of such trouble than Nigel Gresley's 1921 Quintuple Dining Set, which we have met before. Because there were five full vehicles in the set, articulated together, any defect in one meant that all five had to come out, be it a broken window, a dragging brake or something equally trivial. To arrive at King's Cross in the morning and find the 'Quin' standing forlornly in a bay made strong men shudder and weak men weaker. All the food, beers, wine, linen, glass and china, cutlery, pots and pans would have to be changed to another set on another platform in half an hour or less; everything then had to be sorted out afresh before breakfast was cooked and prepared for up to 200 hungry passengers, all demanding to know the reason for the delay.

There is no 'Quin' today, and maintenance is simpler, but the intensive use of train sets has reduced layover time and the sets are much more likely to be transposed if the incoming working is late. This poses little problem to driver, guard and passengers but the restaurant car crew is still faced with moving piles of stores, maybe right across a big station at a few moments' notice, and the reception they receive when meal service is delayed is no more pleasant than of yore. Sometimes there is only time to transfer a few cases of beer and sandwiches, and the resulting 'buffet only' service is guaranteed to generate letters to management and newspapers as well as hard words to the crew.

Complaints are inevitable in such a complex business, but many have their lighter side and some are avoided at the last minute through frantic hard work by the staff concerned. One summer's day a Boy Scouts' Association special was booked, and as it was to be a buffet service, the crew placed orders at the depot for lots of minerals, Coca-cola, and crisps. In the words of the manager on duty, 'the party did not get to the platform until just before the off and oh, calamity! they were all Commissioners, District Officers and the like – all grown-ups and in many cases with their wives.' But after a bit of a panic the necessary provender was substituted, and all ultimately was well.

Rather the same sort of thing happened a considerable time ago, when church parties travelling by train were not uncommon. A special party had been booked with the letters WMC, which were taken to mean Wesleyan Methodist Chapel, and as it was known that the Methodists were teetotal, the order of the day was soft drinks. The run was from Nottingham to Blackpool, and when the restaurant car staff booked on at Nottingham that morning they found themselves confronted by the hefty members of a Working Men's Club, all wanting plenty of beer for breakfast. Luckily a sense of humour prevailed, and proper supplies were obtained at Blackpool for the return trip; but the lesson was learned that guesses are not good business.

But one day in the height of summer in the late 1930s, a party 120 strong booked onto the 11.00am Edinburgh to King's Cross express. This was a very busy train for lunches, even without large parties, and a lodging turn as well. The crew had worked north the previous day with the encouraging remark from the manager, 'you'll be all right with the 120 party, they're a school, and you'll be able to fix them three to a double seat.' The following evening the manager went down to the platform to meet the train. The staff were on their knees; they had served 350 lunches. For the first time the manager saw what no-one had told him; the school was a mountaineering school – 'they were all big and husky, like Vikings,' he lamented, 'and was my face red!'

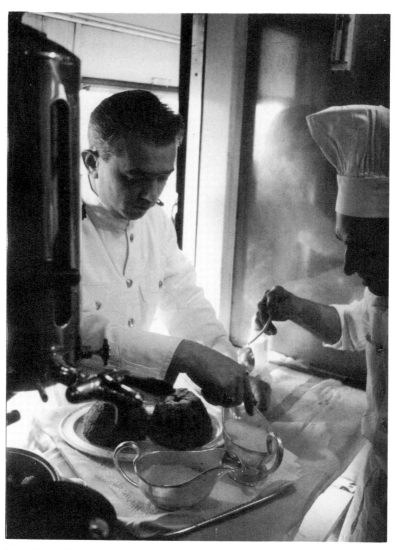

'That's yer lot, mate!' The bustle behind the scenes, captured on a West Coast express about 1963. *British Rail.*

Before the days of plastic containers, detergent for washing-up was issued from bulk supply in the stores. It went out in non-returnable wine bottles from which the labels were supposed to have been removed – at least, that was the theory. If a label was perchance left on, the staff would still recognise it –

that was another theory. Well, one day a certain conductor who liked to finish any wine left by a passenger took a good swig at a bottle and immediately started foaming at the mouth. He had grabbed the detergent bottle by mistake. But there were grave suspicions of a 'plant' by members of his own crew . . .

Bad packing of stores was a considerable problem in pre-plastic days when plain bags sometimes carried no labels. On one High Tea Special train, the salt cellars were inadvertantly filled with caster sugar and the sugar casters with salt. It seems hard to believe that all 200 passengers spoilt their plaice and chips with sugar and shook salt all over their sweet, but that was the claim made by the party organiser, and the management deemed it wise not to argue too much and to lop the demanded amount off the bill.

By and large, restaurant car staff humour their passengers, though there are occasions when a slightly barbed leg-pull comes in useful. Not so long ago a finger-clicking, 'waiter'-shouting young excutive, trying to impress his two girl companions, irritated a steward on the Wolverhampton run so much that he decided to play a trick. 'When it came to the cheese,' the steward recalled, 'I unwrapped a slab of butter and put it on the board. I knew he'd say, "This is Stilton, and this is Brie," and he did. When he came to the butter, he said to the girls, "This is Lancashire," and I said, "No, that's butter, Sir". But I only made a fool of him because he'd tried to make one of me.'

But we will let the last word on life on the cars be with a Euston steward, who became concerned one night when a teenage girl came up to his buffet bar and consumed several large whiskies very quickly. Business was slack and the two got talking, but soon the girl declared she was going to have one more and then throw herself off the train. The steward elicited that she had just been turned down by the married man she loved, and with a little psychology and fatherly chat he had her feeling considerably better by the time the train reached its destination. 'In the buffet bar,' he said, 'when you're by yourself, people tell you things they wouldn't tell their friends, because they probably won't see you again. It's a funny situation, being on a train together.'

9
Food and Drink

For more than half a century the first express of the day from Leeds to King's Cross has been known throughout West Yorkshire as 'The Breakfast Train.' Businessman, socialite, politician or student – one and all regard it as one of life's institutions, and though the departure time may have varied a little one side or the other of half-past seven, the special atmosphere of this crack service has remained as strong as ever. There are other breakfast trains to London from provincial cities, but nothing quite like the seven-thirty from Leeds.

By 1967 bookings had become so heavy that a second Yorkshire breakfast train, 07.20 from Bradford, was introduced, and with a stop at the new 'park-and-ride' station of New Pudsey, British Rail aimed to tap the market from northern and western Yorkshire and relieve pressure on the older-established service. The breakfast, of course, was the same, and the Eastern Region restaurant car department took care to roster some of its best staff to the new train.

But Yorkshire habits die hard, and for a long time the loading on the Bradford train remained embarrassingly light, while the Leeds remained as crowded as ever. One morning, a chance conversation overheard by the writer shed a little light on this. As the Leeds train sped through the South Yorkshire coalfields in the half-light of a winter's dawn, two West Riding businessmen addressed mouth-watering platefuls from the grill tray. 'You come in from Ilkley, Jim,' said the first. 'Wouldn't you find it more convenient to get t'other train from New Pudsey?' There was a pause while bacon was munched, and then Jim, jabbing his fork at his plate, observed: 'Y' get more mooshrooms on this 'un.'

Bacon, fried egg, sausage, tomato, fried bread, mushrooms and sauté potatoes have been the mainstay of the railway breakfast for generations. Few other places can regularly be counted on to serve such a generous plateful. Some things about it have an unexpectedly practical twist; with the silver service used on restaurant cars, the most skilled steward finds it easier to serve a succession of fried eggs unbroken with a triangle of fried bread safely under each. But there is nothing mystical about the top quality ingredients. Even today, many passengers swear they cannot buy bacon as good as that served on the trains, and ask what it is. It is best Dutch back bacon, smoked, and specially packed for British Rail.

Equally hallowed is the traditional kipper – a special joy on the breakfast train, if only because the smell of their cooking does not encourage the housewife to serve kippers at home. The British custom is to serve kippers by the pair – something kept up to this day on the trains. The meal is rounded-off with liberal supplies of steaming coffee. This has a history, too. Starting in 1920 the Midland Railway, followed by the LMS and then BR, ground and blended its own distinctive coffee in the cavernous cellars under St Pancras station. This mystic brew, much revered (unlike buffet car coffee) by the *cognoscenti*, was supplied in its heyday to all the railway hotels and ships, as well as restaurant cars. Four different coffees went into the blend: four parts each of Kenya and Santos (from Brazil), and one each of Mocha (from Ethiopia) and Old Brown Indonesia ('OBI') from Java. For many years the blending was in the loving charge of a West Indian, George Jean-Baptiste, whose 'nose' for the brew was all-important for fine adjustment in the mixing. George used to wax lyrical about his beans: 'The LMS always took pride in the pungency of its cigars and its private blend of coffee. Take the OBI coffee beans – they make a very heavy, rich liquor. Before the War the Dutch kept the beans for eight years before selling them, and the weevil-holes in the beans were living proof of their age.'

The subterranean roasting and grinding of all these beans caused a quite delicious aroma to drift up through the gratings around St Pancras forecourt, and local passers-by became so addicted that they frequently made detours through the station precincts to sniff their 'fix.' Sadly, the machinery for the job became rather unreliable in later years, notably the gas-fired roaster, the heat from which regularly caused conflagrations in the chimney vents where fine coffee dust built up. On such occasions, the chimney would suddenly deluge the neighbourhood with puffs of acrid blue smoke, prompting reports, it is said, that a new stationmaster had been elected at St Pancras. With the equipment needing costly renovation, and the railway hotels being sold off, this fascinating operation came to a sad but inevitable end in 1983; British Rail today buys coffee based on the old brew, but old-timers understandably assert that it is not quite the same.

The Great British Breakfast with its distinctive coffee may be the favourite railway meal, but other traditions also flourish, that seem in danger of extinction elsewhere. At afternoon tea time, the restaurant car remains one of the last bastions of the toasted teacake, while aunts and grannies in particular appreciate the traditional offering of fresh, crisp celery with the cheese at lunch and dinner.

A great variety of social and regional tastes sit at the dining car table, and a straightfoward menu, simple to prepare and acceptable to all, is the best and most practical approach. Nevertheless, individual cooks vary in their abilities and inclinations, and certain trains have down the years acquired certain reputations. One of these in the 1960s and early 1970s was the 18.00 from King's Cross to Newcastle, where the regular cook had a speciality known to East Coast travellers as 'Eighteen-Hundred Steak and Kidney Pie,' which was usually available even if not officially on the menu. The first stop of this train was Darlington, but a number of York passengers used to catch it deliberately and then wait for a local service back to York, just so as to partake of this rich and glorious dish. If challenged by a travelling ticket inspector, these diners would swear blind they thought the train stopped at York, appearing most upset when told they faced a wait at Darlington and then a 40-minute trip back. The exact recipe for this siren dish remained a closely-guarded secret, but the cook did once vouchsafe to the writer that a generous measure of sweet sherry, not strictly in the cooks' manual, had something to do with it.

Steak and kidney pie is one of those things that has changed little down the ages, but the actual menus have altered considerably along with fashions and changing food prices. The tracing of these changes is a fascinating study. When third class dining began in Queen Victoria's last decade first and third class passengers were offered different menus as well as sitting in different carriages. A sample Great Northern Railway menu set of 1898 shows the first class table d'hôte luncheon at 2s 6d (12½p), consisting of five courses: Printanier (a clear vegetable soup), grilled turbot, roast sirloin and vegetables, bread and butter pudding, and cheese, with coffee 4d (2p) extra. The third class lunch, costing 2s 0d (10p), merely lacked the fish course. But at dinner the gap between the classes widened. The 3s 6d (17½p) first class meal offered seven courses – soup, salmon with sauce Hollandaise, lamb cutlet, roast chicken, salad and sweet (offered together), cheese, and dessert – whereas for a full shilling (5p) less the third class got five courses – soup, boiled cod and oyster sauce, roast leg of mutton, sweet, and cheese.

Meal prices varied little until the economic havoc of the Great Depression set in in the early 1930s. Youngsters ate at reduced

A Caledonian Railway menu of 1897, as served on through West Coast expresses to London, one of which bore the diner (according to the note) on a trip to Queen Victoria's Diamond Jubilee celebrations. The half-crown (12½p) dinner would, if raised in line with the Retail Price Index, cost £4.25 in 1986. *Author's collection.*

WEST COAST DINING SALOON.

Third Class Dinner, 2/6

18th J U N E , 1897

C. R.

Menu.

Green Pea Soup
Roast Sirloin of Beef
Cabbage   New Potatoes
Cabinet Pudding   ·
Maraschino Ice

Cheese, Butter, etc

A LA CARTE.

Macaroni Soup. 6d
Pressed Beef, 1/3
Cold Pie, 1/9   Galantine, 1/3
Chicken and Ham. 1/9
Grilled Chicken and Ham, 1/9
Grilled Steak. 1/6   Chop, 1/6
Compote of Fruit and Rice, 6d

Cup of Tea or Coffee with Luncheon
or Dinner, 3d.

prices. GWR menus of the 1920s, for example, show 'children's meals' (age not specified) at half-price, though by 1931 this concession had apparently been withdrawn. Today it applies very specifically to those under 11, for youngsters from their pre-teens upwards are known to be some of the hungriest eaters around!

The actual dishes on offer in the old days are fascinating too, but distance lends enchantment and some of them do not sound too appetising to today's palate. A West Coast line menu dated June 1897, for instance, begins with macaroni soup, which proves, from an old cookery book, to be little more than seasoned stock with pieces of macaroni floating in it. Third class menus were often long on boiled this and that, cabbage, and custard, the best bet usually being a chop or steak, both of which were equally popular at the turn of the century and which, as we have noted before, were served on some lines as a lighter, one-course offering between set mealtimes.

In 1925 the total food consumed on Britain's dining cars, according to a *Railway Magazine* article of the day, included 965 tons of meat and no less than 779 tons of fish. The British have progressively lost their taste for fresh fish. The species too have changed; turbot, for example, is very seldom encountered today, while halibut, another favourite fifty years ago, has become prohibitively expensive. So too have oysters, once made into sauce to dress the poor man's boiled cod!

On the meat plate, beef was as popular then as it is now, though pork, eschewed by some for religious reasons, has seldom featured on any menu. But while today's diner will often encounter roast lamb, his grandfather would invariably order mutton (the same animal but older), with a coarser texture maybe, but much more flavour. Roast mutton with onion sauce – a simple but delicious accompaniment, all but forgotten today – has deserted the restaurant car as it has the domestic dining room. Poultry, that other mainstay of the main course, has likewise changed; chicken, by reason of intensive farming, is now much more plentiful and relatively cheaper, whereas the once-popular capon might well produce the reaction 'What?' from today's passenger.

Goose, a menu regular until well after World War II, now seldom appears at the family Christmas table, let alone in the restaurant car. Weight for weight, he is not an economic bird for

Plum pudding, mince pies and crackers under the paper chains on the LMS Royal Scot, Christmas 1932. *BBC Hulton Picture Library.*

catering, but before the turkey usurped his place he had a wide following. Goose can be tough and needs careful preparation, and his very presence on the menu could be enough to set the restaurant car 'jokes' rolling in. In the dark days of 1949 a *Yorkshire Post* reporter asked his companion what his plate of poultry was like. 'Leather!' came the laconic reply. 'Alleged to be a goose, but I think this must be a pigeon they've killed on the line. Poor thing, probably too old to get out of way. Gets worse, doesn't it?'.

Both goose and turkey starred in what for many was the high point of the restaurant car service – the Christmas dinner of the 1930s. By that time rail was the transport of the masses but private motor travel was still the privilege of the better-off, so the crowds of rail passengers at Christmastide were of true Bank Holiday proportions. The holiday period itself was far shorter in those days, with a full programme of train services throughout and a recognisable main line timetable on Christmas Day itself.

Menu

L.M.S. RESTAURANT CAR.

Luncheon

3/6

Tomato Soup

——

Fried Slip Sole & Lemon

——

Roast Turkey & Sausage
Baked & Boiled Potatoes
Savoy Cabbage

or

Assorted Cold Meats
Salad

——

Christmas Pudding
Mince Pie

——

Cheese, Salad, etc.

——

Coffee, per Cup, 4d.

XMAS DAY 1932.

Beer, also high on Head's Wolverton list, may have come close to being the ruin of refreshment rooms in late Victorian times, but nearly a hundred years later it was to pay back its debt in a rather unlikely way. During the 1960s real ale drawn by hand pump had been all but killed-off by keg beers in the pubs of Britain, but at Lincoln Central Station, British Rail chalked up a notable record when loyal traditionalist Miss Holt became the last refreshment room manageress to serve the real stuff. She was still serving it in 1975 when Travellers-Fare, as it was by then, decided to capitalise on the very newsworthy real ale revival with its national chain of free houses and their ideal Victorian cellars. As the London *Evening News* had it in March 1976:

> 'St Pancras Station on a wet night has traditionally fallen well behind strip clubs, night spots, theatres and bed as a spot of evening entertainment. Now all that has changed. It has emerged quite suddenly as a trendy meeting place for *bon vivants*, many of whom would not recognise the sound of an approaching train if they laid their ear on the line. And it is Real Ale that has done it.'

The real ale enthusiast since then has found railway stations a happy hunting ground. Recently, though, he has been waging something of a war of words against the encroachment of lager into British beer-drinking – so hark to *The Daily Telegraph* as far back as 11 May 1906, no less, which picked up the trend 80 years ealier:

> 'The public insists on lighter refreshments than formerly. Heavy beers like stout have given place to lager, the port and sherry days are over, and light claret has become the favourite wine.'

A battle unlikely ever to be won is that to serve real ale on trains successfully. While a number of today's preserved railways 'cheat' by using party polypins, there was a serious attempt in 1948 to bring in the real thing on the Southern Region of BR. On the counter of several buffet cars there proudly appeared a cask of Ind Coope & Allsopp's Bitter. But problems quickly arose with the motion of the train – especially across all those junctions on the Southern lines – which made for a very murky pint. Another hazard was stock control. When buffet crews change over, takings have to be balanced against stock sold. In the absence of modern meters, the measuring was done

The steward guards his cask of Ind Coope bitter in the prison-like surroundings of a Waterloo – Exeter buffet car, April 1948. *British Rail.*

Manchester (Exchange) refreshment room in 1885. Diners are clearly expected at table, while the buffet counter offers Bath buns, Abernethy biscuits, sandwiches in bell jars, and boxes of Fry's Nougat Sticks. *Crown Copyright. National Railway Museum, York.*

by poking a home-made wooden dipstick in through the cask spile hole, but this system lent itself to all sorts of skulduggery, let alone what it might have done to the beer. Sadly, but not surprisingly, the experiment came to an early end.

The 'revival' of refreshment rooms, of which more in our final chapter, reminds us that in their earliest days, despite the strictures of Dickens and others, these places did bring to the public notice some tasty regional specialities which otherwise might have lived and died in provincial obscurity. One such dates from the opening of the Liverpool & Manchester Railway in 1830, when Eccles cakes, those round sugary pastries with currants and candied peel, went on sale at a house calling itself 'The noted Eccles Cake Shop,' next to Eccles Station. Eccles cakes are still widely available in the North of England, but it is

less easy to track down another former railway favourite, Banbury cakes, with their mincemeat filling and distinctive lozenge shape. In proof of their fame and provenance, the 1934 GWR timetable carried this notice: 'Banbury cakes, made from the best and purest ingredients: obtainable from E. W. Brown, The Original Cake Shop, Banbury, and at GWR Refreshment Rooms.'

Another bun of note, less common today, was the Bath bun, which the writer Ashley Sterne described in *The Globe* magazine of March 1920 as 'deserving to form an honourable triumvirate along with British beef and British beer, which two, as is now recognised, have made England what she is today.' But Sterne goes on: 'Yet the subtle appeal of the Bath bun is hard to define. It has no suggestion of the medicinal waters of Bath about it, nor – except at railway buffets – any reminiscence of the Bath brick.'

The hardness and staleness of bread and buns, which pervaded the writings of buffet commentators for so long, was largely the fault of the old-fashioned bell jar, once the only practical form of protecting food. These now-vanished utensils may have just about kept the flies off, but airtight they were not, and in the days before cling wrapping the consequences were inevitable. Bell jars must have positively enhanced the rock-like qualities of the old-fashioned Abernethy biscuit, which a writer in the *Walsall Recorder* back in 1906 described as 'not often seen today.' This biscuit, he tells us, was 'baked very hard and flavoured with caraway seeds.' There was much hilarity at Walsall refreshment room when he made to buy one, and one of the serving girls giggled, 'You're not going to eat it yourself? You'll break every tooth in your head!' 'There was nothing exceptional about the biscuit,' he concluded, 'but dental degeneration has become so common that the average man's teeth are not equal to a well-conditioned Abernethy.'

Despite the problems of keeping things fresh, there were brave attempts down the years to please in the manner of sandwiches and snacks, one early example being that of the LNWR which in 1906 mounted a special selection of French sandwiches in the Euston booking-hall buffet. The range, priced

(*Opposite*)
A GWR refreshment room tariff of 1909, with different prices for first and second class passengers, third class, and railway staff. *Travellers Fare.*

GREAT WESTERN RAILWAY.

Hotels and Refreshment Rooms Department.

TARIFF.

	1ST AND 2ND CLASS.	3RD CLASS.	COMPANY'S SERVANTS.
BREAKFASTS OR TEAS.			
Pot of Tea, Coffee or Cocoa, with Bread & Butter or Toast, Cake & Preserves (ad lib.) each per.	1/0	9d.	9d.
,, ,, ,, ,, ,, 2 Eggs ,, ,, or Toast and Preserves ,, ,,	1/6	1/3	1/0
,, ,, ,, ,, ,, Ham and Eggs, Chop or Steak, including Bread and Butter or Toast, and Preserves ... ... each person	2/0	1/6	1/6
LUNCHEON.			
Soup, per plate, including Bread ...	9d.	6d.	6d.
Cold Meat, with Pickles, Vegetables, Bread, Butter, Cheese and Salad (ad lib.) each per.	1/6	1/6	1/6
Cold Chicken with Ham, Pickles, Vegetables, Bread, Butter, Cheese and Salad (ad lib.)	2/0	2/0	2/0
Portion of Cold Meat or Ham, with Bread & Butter (small plate) at counter [each per.	8d.	8d.	8d.
Portion of Cold Chicken and Ham, including Bread (small plate) at counter ...	1/3	1/3	1/3
Bovril, with Bread, etc. ... ... per Cup	4d.	4d.	4d.
Chicken, Ham and Tongue Sausage, with Bread and Butter ... ... per Plate	8d.	8d.	8d.
DINNERS.			
Hot Joints, with Vegetables, Bread, Butter, Cheese and Salad (ad lib.) each person	2/0	—	1/6
(Soup or Fish, 6d. extra ; Sweets, 4d.)			
SUNDRIES.			
Sandwiches ... ... each	2d.	2d.	2d.
,, Boxes containing 3 for 6d. ; 6 for 1/-			
Roll and Butter	2d.	2d.	2d.
Hard-Boiled Eggs ... ... each	3d.	3d.	2d.
Sardines on Toast	6d.	6d.	6d.
Meat Pasties	6d.	6d.	4½d.
Tea, Coffee or Cocoa, freshly made ... ... per Cup	3d.	2d.	1½d.
,, ,, ,, with Two Slices of Bread and Butter	4d.	3d.	2½d.
Pot of Tea or Coffee, ,, ,, ,, ,, ,, each person	6d.	4d.	3d.
New Milk ... ... per Glass	2d.	1½d.	1½d.
,, ,, ... ,, ½ ,,	—	—	1d.
Biscuits, Plain Buns, Cheesecakes, Queen Cakes, Sponge Cakes ... each	1d.	1d.	1d.
Banbury Cakes, Bath Buns, Sausage Rolls, Tarts, Slices of Cake ... ,,	2d.	2d.	2d.
Bread and Cheese ... ... ,,	3d.	3d.	2d.
Sausages ... ... ,,	3d.	3d.	3d.
AERATED WATERS.			
Soda Water, Lemonade, Seltzer, or Ginger Beer ... ... per Bottle	3d.	3d.	2d.
,, ,, ,, ,, ,, per Small ,,	2d.	2d.	2d.
Apollinaris or Schweppes Soda or Ginger Ale ... ... per ,,	6d.	6d.	6d.
Schweppes Split Soda or Ginger Ale	3d.	3d.	3d.
ALES. &c.			
Bitter or Mild ... ... per Glass	2d.	2d.	1½d.
Stout ... ... ,,	2d.	2d.	1½d.
Bass' Ale or Guinness' Stout (Bottled) ... ... Reputed Pint	6d.	6d.	6d.
,, ,, ,, ,, ,, ... Impl. ½ ,,	4d.	4d.	4d.
Cider and Pilsener Lager Beer ... ... Reputed ,,	6d.	6d.	6d.
Small Lager Beer	4d.	4d.	4d.
WINES.			
Port, Sherry, Claret, or Ginger Wine ... ... per Glass	4d. & 6d.	4d. & 6d.	4d. & 6d.
Claret (per Half-Bottle) ... ... from	1/0	1/0	1/0
SPIRITS.			
Whisky (Scotch or Irish), Gin, Hollands, or Rum ... ... per Measure	4d. & 6d.	4d.	4d.
Brandy ... ... ,, ,,	4d. & 6d.	4d. & 6d.	4d. & 6d.
Whisky (Canadian Club) ... ... ,, ,,	6d.	6d.	6d.
Whisky (Irish or Scotch), Special Brands ... ... ,, ,,	6d.	6d.	6d.
Brandy, Liqueur ... ... ,, ,,	9d.	9d.	9d.
LIQUEURS.			
Bénédictine, Curaçoa, Maraschino, Noyeau, Cherry Brandy, Ginger Brandy, Sloe Gin, Chartreuse ... ... per Liqueur Glass.	9d.	9d.	9d.
CORDIALS.			
Lime Juice ... ... per Sherry Glass	2d. & 3d.	2d. & 3d.	2d. & 3d.

NOTE.—Any attendant exhibiting this Tariff will be liable to dismissal. The third column applies only to *bonâ-fide* employees of the Company, and great care must be taken to check all sales at these reduced prices.

S. D. BUOTT,
Manager of Hotels, Refreshment Rooms and Dining Cars Department,
Paddington Station, London, W.

May 18, 1909.

250.—W. 170—5-09.

from 2d to 4d, included caviar, anchovy, foie gras, smoked salmon (in white or brown bread), prawn and shrimp, as well as tried and trusted items like egg and cress. A *Daily Telegraph* reporter took himself over to Liverpool Street, to see how the Great Eastern were competing, but was curtly informed: 'The favourite "snack" of the passenger at Liverpool Street is the crisply-baked ham sandwich, and kickshaws are neither asked for nor supplied.' This may have reflected the more workaday tastes of travellers on the east side of London, but it is also true that until quite recently anything more adventurous than the inevitable ham, cheese, egg, or tomato sold so few as to make it not worthwhile preparing them.

The Paddington Quick Lunch Bar of 1936 described earlier took particular aim at a more sophisticated market with 'Paddington 3-deckers', consisting of smoked ham, lettuce and mayonnaise at 2s 0d (10p) (more than half the price of a restaurant car meal!), tongue, gruyère cheese and tomato at 1s 3d (6p), or ham, cheese and tomato at 1s 2d. Tongue and gruyère are no longer so fashionable; their counterparts today would probably be paté and Brie. At about the same time milk bars, also described earlier, were beginning to appear at places like Leeds and Hull, where the menu made a special feature of favourites like Horlicks, Ovaltine, and Bourn-Vita.

Some of the staple offerings of refreshment rooms used to be on sale to railway staff at lower than public prices. This was a real 'perk' for employees where other eating places were few or expensive. A GWR tariff of 1909 shows worthwhile reductions on hot plated meals – 2s 0d (10p) down to 1s 6d (7½p); there was 1d off soda water or lemonade, and ½d off a glass of beer. But a printed note warned refreshment room staff that this dual tariff was on no account to be shown to the public, and any member of staff displaying it did so on pain of dismissal!

Fascinating though these half-forgotten dishes may be, it has to be said that British food in High Street and hotel as well as on the line was for long not exactly famed for flair and imagination. Where the railways could excel, as in their hotels or on special occasions, they did. Otherwise, it was to be well into the 1970s before the bad old days truly began to disappear on a wide scale. First, the means of this happening had to be set up – and that is our final chapter.

10
Fare for Today

As he took his place at his desk on the morning of 1 October 1953
E. K. Portman-Dixon, appointed under the new Transport Act to
head the whole of Britain's railway catering, faced a massive
task. Over the previous five years, despite politics, prejudice and
trading problems, he had made much progress in putting British
Railways' refreshment rooms into better shape; now he
confronted an even more daunting challenge with the
restaurant cars.

One of his most pressing problems was the elderly state of the
vehicles themselves – the 'Age of the Train', as a later railway
slogan unwittingly enshrined it. Robustly built to carry heavy
ranges, refrigerators and other kitchen ware, restaurant cars
easily outlived most other passenger carriages. Faced with the
very high costs of building new catering vehicles, most
companies had rebuilt these hardy old soldiers, in some cases
several times over, so that of Portman-Dixon's inherited fleet of
727 no fewer than 135 were more than 30 years old, with 477 –
fully two-thirds of the total – twenty years old or more. Only 69,
running on the most important main-line expresses, were of
post-war vintage.

British Railways was now embarking on a massive
programme for building a range of new standardised passenger
rolling stock – the BR Mark I stock – and sensibly, the dining car
staff themselves were called in to help design the new catering
vehicles. There was great scope for economy by standardising
equipment, while new general-purpose designs would allow the
total fleet to be cut by over 120 cars. In 1956, the first of the
standard prototypes appeared, and thereafter a rolling
programme totalling 420 vehicles in all continued to come out of
Works, finishing in 1962. A dozen of the earliest were full

A British Railways Mk I Miniature Buffet Car, as new in 1960. *British Rail.*

kitchen cars devoted entirely to working space, but most were a mixture of kitchen and passenger accommodation. A large batch of these were restaurant-buffets, with a small kitchen, a bar next to it and a seating area beyond. These were (and are) very versatile, but the snag was that stewards trying to serve the seated passengers were obliged to pick their way through the crowd round the bar. The meal-takers meanwhile complained that the noise and smoke from the bar did not mix well with their food. The solution was to serve the full meals into an ordinary saloon coach marshalled next to the kitchen end of the 'RB', as it was known. Thus arranged, some of these vehicles continue to give yeoman service today – heavily refurbished, true, but still basically a quarter of a century old.

Kitchen buffets had their cramped bar area and once-familiar 'Maypole' drinks stand, while what were basically light refreshment kiosks in second class saloon vehicles went by the name of 'Miniature Buffet.' This name soon found its way into official railway publicity, and station announcers would repeat the theme: 'The 10.39 to Leeds and Manchester conveys a miniature Buffet Car', leading puzzled passengers to expect the train to roll in with a Hornby Dublo vehicle in its formation. But one type of catering car notably absent from the new building plans was the cafeteria car, familiar at that time on the 'Starlight Specials' and other holiday trains; passengers were taking so long choosing from the self-service cabinets that massive queues built up, completely blocking the corridor to all comers for a coach length and more.

One rather special new vehicle was the Griddle Car, like the Miniature Buffet an idea developed by Portman-Dixon himself. Its main attraction was the fondly-remembered Aberdeen Angus Steaklet, cooked to order in under two minutes on a specially-designed propane gas griddle plate – a first step towards today's world of fast food. The inside of these cars was particularly attractive, but the design demanded at least two staff to work them – a telling disadvantage, as they were intended for lines where loadings were light and economical staffing was essential. The Griddles found their niche in the Scottish Highlands, where some of the most elderly of the old companies' restaurant cars had by the 1960s been put out to grass. Passengers appreciated the Griddles and the new order, but many were reluctant to see the old-stagers go. There had been something irresistible about moving through pass and glen at a stately 40mph, seated in an old 1920s LMS twelve-wheeler, with passengers half-expecting the steward to appear with a gun over one shoulder and fishing-rod over the other, and the query, 'Salmon or grouse, Sir?'

With the huge Mark I building programme complete, the average 'age of the train' was now very much younger, so for a full 13 years while the following Mark II programme was under way no new restaurant or buffet cars were built at all. But meanwhile the railways were demanding much higher productivity from all their resources, which meant all the cars being used much more intensively. Train speeds were rising too, especially with the electrification of the West Coast Main Line, and the Mark I catering cars began to show signs of age much earlier than their predecessors had done. Various partial refurbishment schemes proved to be very much cases of new wine in old bottles. With no new cars coming off the production line and the Inter-City 125s with their Mk III cars not yet on the drawing board, the old Mk I workhorses, ever game but more and more unreliable, now provided a new cause for public complaint and another opening for the ever-lurking media cynics.

The West Coast Main Line, as we have seen before, had ever been Britain's most important catering route, and the London Midland Region was thus predominant in the train catering organisation. Indeed, for a time in the mid-1960s there was one operating manager in the organisation for the London Midland, and one for the whole of the rest of England and Wales. The Scottish Region, an entirely new entity for the railways created in 1948, was considered not to merit its own train catering manager and right up until the 1980s shared one with the refreshment rooms.

Another significant move at this time was the gradual takeover of the Pullman empire. Pullman, as we saw earlier, had originated train catering in Britain but had then developed on a separate course, maintaining its status as a private contractor. With Nationalisation, the emphasis had shifted away from contractors towards in-house services and in 1954 the British Transport Commission bought out all the ordinary shares of Pullman, though the company still continued to operate independently. The second stage of the takeover came in 1962 when the BTC bought all the preference shares. On 1 January 1963 Dr Richard Beeching, Chairman of the newly formed British Railways Board, re-established Pullman as a Division of British Transport Hotels Ltd., reporting to its General Manager, Frank Hole. Just three months later Pullman lost further identity when it was placed under the BTH rail catering chief, Portman-Dixon. The final stage of integration took place on 14 March 1967, when the Pullman Division was fully merged into the restaurant car departments of the British Rail regions. The Pullman Car Company itself, however, was never officially wound up, and remains technically a wholly-owned subsidiary of the BRB.

Over its 90-year history the Pullman tradition of excellence had fostered something of a special spirit in the company's employees, and as they became swallowed up by the more workaday railway catering service there was a certain amount of natural resentment at what must have seemed a considerable loss of status. Among railway staff there was some corresponding ill-feeling at the way these 'superior beings' came in, taking it seemed the most convenient workings, the handiest sidings, the fastest turn-rounds and even getting railway staff to handle their refuse. As a contemporary observer put it, 'We attempted to find wherefrom came the "Pull" in Pullman, but all we found was a blank wall!'

One product of the Pullman re-think of those times was the Blue Pullman trains. There were five of these splendid diesel multiple-units – three eight-car sets (one spare) on the Western Region, and two six-car sets (one spare) on the London Midland. The Midland set began operating in July 1960 from Manchester Central to St Pancras in the morning and back in the evening, with a fill-in turn to Leicester and back in the middle of the day. This mid-day turn proved lightly loaded, and from 2 October 1961 was extended to Nottingham. But this seemingly harmless move stirred up a hornet's nest. The Pullman preference shares were at this time still privately owned, and the National Union of Railwaymen, politically keen to have Pullman fully absorbed as soon as possible, saw the whole thing instead as a further and dangerous invasion of their territory by the private sector. Affairs quickly came to a head and on the first scheduled day of the new workings the attendants blacked the Nottingham leg of the diagram, working between Manchester and St Pancras only. This blacking continued amid some acrimony until 30 November, by which time it had been widely reported as the first industrial action ever to affect Pullman in Britain.

The Blue Pullmans were an attractive way to travel, but they had a comparatively short reign. The Midland Pullman was superseded in 1966 by the new Manchester Pullman running between Manchester Piccadilly and Euston on the newly-electrified line; those on the Western continued into the 1970s until replaced in turn by the Inter-City 125s. These used the new, longer Mk III coaches and their general standard of comfort, in particular in the first class, came close to making the Pullman concept redundant; no further Pullmans were built, and for several years up to 1985 the Manchester Pullman was left as Britain's sole surviving Pullman train.

It was the activities of the privately-owned Venice Simplon Orient Express, with its vintage Pullman coaches rescued from scrapyards and lovingly restored, which re-kindled public interest in Pullman as a world of superior cuisine and service as well as comfort and tradition. The May 1985 timetable saw a re-launch of Pullman on both East and West Coast main lines, and railway catering staff manned all these services. There was now a new addition to the luxury service – Pullman Lounges at certain major termini, the first of which were managed by Travellers-Fare's station catering division. Pullman had always hitherto confined itself to operations on board trains, and the lounges thus represented its first totally new venture after 111 years of service in Britain.

The set-up into which Pullman became absorbed had by now evolved somewhat. Back in 1948 train and station catering were two somewhat junior strands of the Hotels Executive. In 1953 they were brought together as part of the new body, British Transport Hotels & Catering Services, with E. K. Portman-Dixon at their head; BTH&CS did not have the powers of the old Executive, but in 1959 it did acquire its own Board of Management, giving it greater independent status. In 1963 came the setting-up of British Transport Hotels Ltd under the new BRB, and the Hotels Board for the first time took on well-known outside caterers as non-executive members, including Charles Forte, later to become Sir Charles of Trust House Forte fame. Meanwhile Portman-Dixon as rail catering chief still reported to the Hotels General Manager, and this caused a wave of disappointment among the more far-sighted in the industry. For railway catering and hotels were moving ever further apart in their markets and activities, and a splendid opportunity had now been missed to place Portman-Dixon and his catering team directly under his logical overlord – the Railways Board. A small step in this direction was in fact taken three years later, when Portman-Dixon, hitherto Chief of Restaurant Cars and Refreshment Rooms, was made general manager (and his organisation renamed British Rail Catering).

For some years after Nationalisation, the Hotel and Catering headquarters remained at Marylebone, first in the former Great Central Hotel and then in the adjoining property No 7 Melbury Terrace. But in 1958 this was knocked down for redevelopment and, after a brief sojourn in the Stephenson Rooms of the old Euston Station, the caterers moved to Carrara House, a modern rented office block under the lee of Charing Cross Bridge on the Embankment. There they remained until 1968 when a further move took place, this time to rejoin the Hotels HQ in St Pancras

Chambers – the former Midland Grand Hotel. By this time Portman-Dixon had retired and his place had been taken by W. J. Currie, brightest of the rising generation of hotel managers.

Hotel background or no, Currie was keen to maintain and increase the momentum of catering away from the hotels organisation. In 1973 British Rail Catering adopted the snappier name Travellers-Fare (a name selected by customers from a list put forward by a marketing consultant), while in 1978 it acquired its own board of directors, independent of the Hotels, and including the well-known restaurateur and food writer Prue Leith. The final split with the Hotels was not to come until 1982 when, with the privatisation of BTH imminent, Travellers-Fare became at last a Division of the British Railways Board. By this time, as we shall see in the closing pages, its managers had set their own course and were fast starting to make up for the time lost, through the legacy of history, over the previous 30 years.

When the first moves towards this end began to take shape in the 1960s, railway catering still physically shared many amenities with the hotels such as the chefs' training courses at New Lodge, Windsor. New Lodge at the time was British Rail's conference and interviewing centre, and guests and residents alike were regaled with a wonderful succession of repasts from the hands of those destined to serve on the Royal Scot or at Gleneagles Hotel. But for railway catering staff the hard reality was very different, nowhere more so than in the refreshment rooms which despite Portman-Dixon's best efforts remained too often unattractive to eat in and unprofitable on the balance sheet. As the effect of the Beeching axe thinned the railway network the losses at many once-important junction stations got worse, and a succession of buffets at such places were closed or let to private tenants. Between late 1954 and Easter 1966 exactly 100 refreshment rooms went this way, including many old-fashioned dining rooms which, just as on the High Street, were losing favour with caterers and customers. It was the beginning of the end for the British three-course meal of brown windsor soup, meat-and-two-veg, and apple pie with thick yellow custard, washed down by diabolical coffee, very milky and none too hot . . .

Travellers-Fare, as it was soon to become, was now concentrating on what the business fraternity might describe as a leaner, fitter portfolio. The new name heralded a new awareness of a need to market railway catering – something foreshadowed by a 1960s poster that showed a perplexed-looking girl sitting in a railway carriage with the caption 'Don't just sit there . . . Eat something.' This poster, widely hailed as the first sign of marketing life in railway catering for a generation or more, drew successfully on the psychologists' assertion that travel produces basic feelings of insecurity in mankind, and insecurity in turn prompts an irresistible urge to nibble and sip. There was indeed an enormous market out there.

Travellers-Fare took on its new identity in 1973 and very soon secured a £5 million grant from the British Railways Board for a massive programme of refreshment room renovation. One of its main thrusts was to get away from the all-purpose station buffet of old, and the first-fruit of this new policy was the Bistro at Liverpool Street in London, which opened in 1973. Situated in two of the Edwardian 'gazebo' tea-rooms which had been knocked into one, the Bistro made the most of its authentic period atmosphere with tasteful decor and furnishings and, most important, a range of continental-style dishes and drinks prepared and served by specially-selected staff. The Bistro was an immediate hit with the crowds from the neighbouring City offices; it was probably the first time Britain had followed the Continental tradition of attracting people into a railway station just to eat. Other bistros at Victoria, Euston and King's Cross, were less successful and did not last the course; the one at Liverpool Street will go sadly but inevitably as the old station is pulled down to make way for its long-overdue replacement.

The next station surprise to spring from the new Travellers-Fare was the wholehearted entry into the real ale revival mentioned previously. From 1976 posters began to appear with slogans such as 'Make your Main Line Station your Local!' Soon upwards of 40 stations up and down the country boasted their hand pumps and their local brew; there were 'Rail Ale Guides' and awards from the Campaign for Real Ale (CAMRA), and a surge of good publicity which the image of the business badly needed. At the same time attention began to turn to profitable retailing, not so much the traditional kiosks with their myriads of low-profit sweets and cigarettes, but off-licences and grocery shops, designed to catch homegoing commuters and other travellers at the big London termini.

Real ale to the fore: a modern view of one of Travellers Fare's most popular ventures, taken in 1982 in the Victoria bar in Marylebone, little changed since 1899. *Travellers Fare.*

For some time station buffets, in an effort to capture some identity, had adopted names of some local or historical feature. These names provided a theme to which interior designers could work. 'The Shires' at St Pancras was one of the first and remains one of the best-known, while 'The Drum' at Waterloo was, and 'The Tournament' at Paddington is, an equally familiar rendezvous. Some of the names however seemed a trifle obscure or contrived. 'The Gauntlet' at Lancaster was so called for no reason other than John of Gaunt's connections with Lancaster Castle nearby. At Bletchley, there is a very small buffet incongruously named 'The Kiln' after the nearby brick fields. But one summer evening a while ago, the writer partook of a sausage roll there. It must have been in the oven throughout a long, hot day, for it had become baked hard and dry, and 'The Kiln' that night seemed remarkably appropriate.

Names apart, several of the buffets made great efforts to mean something more to the local community than the unattractive sandwich bar of legend. Much depended on the personality of the local manageress, which could turn the most boring buffet into a lively meeting point and vice-versa. Though tariffs were dictated from London, there was scope for touches like home cooking; Shrewsbury became famous for its scones, while bread-and-butter pudding, very popular in the North, usefully finished up the crusts from the previous day's sandwiches. But the position of the rooms on the station often did not help, and neither did the position of the station in the town. Buffets on island platforms pulled in little business other than railway users (and railway staff). Those opening onto the street or forecourt were luckier, though the location of many just off the town centre was no help in the age of road transport. Latter-day visitors to places like Lincoln Central must have smiled at the notice allowing it to 'sell intoxicating liquors from three to four o'clock in the afternoon on each and every Friday, excepting Good Friday.' Friday is market day in Lincoln and these powers, though not actually invoked for many years past, were a reminder of the days when the life of the market would be tied inextricably to rail transport.

Curiosities like this remind us that the English liquor licensing laws, so lax in the early days, swung to the other extreme at the time of World War I, and despite a radically-changed society have remained highly restrictive ever since. Today there are signs that long-overdue change may at last be on the way. This owes much to the successful Scottish licensing law reform of 1976, which permits licensees to apply for 'regular extensions' and in effect provides all-day opening. This relaxation was found to improve the old problem of Scottish bibulousness, rather than the opposite which some had feared. It led in Glasgow particularly to a sudden mushrooming of new, comfortable lounge and cocktail bars, where unlike the old street corner taverns, both sexes could enjoy a leisurely drink in attractive surroundings. Travellers-Fare fortuitously had ideal sites for such places at both Central and Queen Street stations, with excellent street frontages, and here they opened the Tropics and Berlin lounge bars, the latter having a discotheque with extremely professional sound and lighting rigged up by the railway signal and telecommunications engineers.

Restored glory: the splendid 1905 Grill Room at Manchester Victoria, as restored 80 years later. *Travellers Fare.*

Sometimes the station buildings themselves formed a useful point of historical interest. One of the best known is the bar at Marylebone in London opened 1899 and scarcely altered inside or out from that day to this. The room forms a perfect backdrop to the real ale scene and in 1978 a redundant dining room next door was cleverly fitted with reproduction bar fittings matching the originals, more than doubling the drinking space. At Victoria Station in Manchester, a considerable sum was spent on sympathetically restoring the fine 'Dome' Grill Room and Bar, first opened by the Lancashire & Yorkshire Railway about 1905 and still retaining all its handsome Edwardian pillars, ceiling and wall finishes. At Carlisle the island platform coffee shop is a well-restored Victorian delight, though unfortunately the old refreshment rooms on the main platform are not now normally accessible to the public. These rooms, in ecclesiastical Tudor by the Victorian architect William Tite, possess stone fireplaces inscribed with the date 1858 in roman numerals, and a series of Latin quotations, one of which translates as 'I will make you always remember this place' – a sinister utterance indeed in the light of the reputation of such places in those days.

Sir William Tite's imposing refreshment room at Carlisle (now a Motorail lounge), seen here about 1953. The fireplace, dated 1858, bears the Latin quotation, *Faciam ut hujus loci semper memineris* (see text). *Travellers Fare*.

Despite all the money and good intentions poured into station catering it was evident by the late 1970s that a bolder initiative would be needed to keep 'market share,' let alone increase it. For the High Street was now offering a choice of Chinese, Indian, Greek and other ethnic eating places, and in particular the American fast food invasion, based on the beefburger, was making itself felt. Fast food seemed to be ideal for station users, many of whom are in a hurry, so a working party was despatched to the United States to study developments there. The result was Casey Jones, Travellers-Fare's own fast food chain, the first of which opened at Waterloo in 1980 and which has now spread to many of the country's biggest stations.

Casey Jones, with its continuous production-line preparation and service, its automated cooking and its colourful, upbeat presentation was an outstanding success from Day 1.

Deliberately marketed without any reference to railways or the name Travellers-Fare, it gave the impression of being a private franchise business and attracted none of the prejudice and cynicism that still dogged traditional railway catering. This breakthrough applied equally to the staff – specially recruited through an advertising campaign which also avoided railway connections, and selected and trained with a new professionalism. For the first time in history, the railway operating managers began to ask their catering counterparts the secrets of their staff selection – a far cry indeed from the portly tea-ladies inherited by Portman-Dixon 40 years earlier.

Bright young career caterers soon found the automation and tightly-controlled systems of Casey Jones rather boring, despite its glamorous side, and began to look for bigger challenges. This meant a very useful spin-off into the more traditional units, themselves now changing to take advantage of Casey Jones-style technology. The last (and possibly one of the best) of the old 'themed' units, the Jazz at Liverpool Street (named after the steam suburban service of the 1920s), had opened in 1981. A professional design studio was responsible for the interior, and with other designers it now competed for work on the new

The first Casey Jones, opened at Waterloo in October 1980. *Travellers Fare.*

generation of coffee shops, 'Quicksnacks' and speciality units coming on stream. These last, such as the Cafe Victoria wine bar in London, again avoided any obvious reference to BR or Travellers-Fare, but many of the new eating places openly flew the house flag and rapidly lifted its image.

The drinking connection carried on with the refitting of the best bars as Station Taverns, and the prevailing political climate prompted some of these to be undertaken as joint ventures with private sector brewery companies, such as at Liverpool Street (east side) and Southend, both totally transformed from a very sleazy previous existence. It was discovered too that pushing these bars very sharply up-market almost entirely solved the problem of the drunks and down-and-outs who had long tarnished the atmosphere of many big station bars.

In 1986 still more new ground was broken with the opening of Food Courts at Euston and Edinburgh Waverley. Here a series of takeaway counters open onto a spacious central eating area which is looked after by specially-trained staff. At Euston one of the counters is operated by private enterprise, and the whole forms a most effective way of offering a wide choice of food while keeping costs to a minimum. The old and the new are cheek-by-jowl at Euston, for on the first floor above the food court stands Carriages, a full table-service restaurant and the very last of the line of station dining rooms that were once a feature of every town.

All this activity meant that station catering, so long the Cinderella of railway hospitality, had not only covered more ground in ten years than it had in the previous hundred; it had also drawn well ahead of train catering in terms of new ideas and new markets. In truth, the stations were batting on a better wicket, for unlike the trains they had remained a profitable business – a status much boosted by the new developments – and thus stood higher in the queue for costly new equipment.

Train catering, meanwhile, had during the 1970s lost a lot of restaurant car trade. Quicker trains, lighter eating habits, and soaring costs passed on in higher prices had combined to reduce the grand total of main meals served from 3½ million in 1973 to around half that number by the end of the decade – a fall not fully counterbalanced by better takings in the buffet car. The business was still apt to be frowned upon as a 'loss-maker' by railway chiefs, while despite the advent of the Inter-City 125s with their new catering vehicles, much of it still operated from unreliable, clapped-out Mk I cars that contrasted badly with the accommodation in the rest of the train. Far from keeping pace with the ever more demanding business travel market, its image seemed to be slipping back. Matters were made even worse by the complete withdrawal of buffet cars from commuter services to places like Hastings and Clacton. This was a railway decision and not a catering one. Such services earned at best a marginal profit, and with the buffet cars worn out it made no economic sense to replace them, using funds vitally needed for more profitable schemes elsewhere. It was a straightforward question of priorities, but a thirsty public was not to be assuaged by such talk. Railway catering ought to run profitably, people argued – unless their own particular glasses were running dry!

All was not entirely gloom, and one bright spark which was to prove a pointer to the future was the train catering Centenary celebrations of 1979. The climax of a summer's festivities was the running that September of a full train of vintage preserved catering cars on a fortnight's tour of Britain. The vehicles, including three Pullmans, came from the National Railway Museum in York, and spanned the years from a 1900 LNWR twelve-wheel first class kitchen diner to one of the BR Scottish griddle cars of 1960 vintage. Staffed by Travellers-Fare, the tour began with a press run from Leeds to King's Cross, re-tracing the route of the former GNR's *Prince of Wales* of 100 years before.

The interest generated by this event was considerable and reinforced a trend that had been gathering steam on the country's preserved railways for some while. This trend, to turn nostalgia into an organised and profitable business, could in the train catering world be traced back to the mid-1950s when the narrow gauge Festiniog Railway, recently reopened in North Wales, converted an 1880-vintage bogie brake van into a buffet saloon, which was really more of a mobile shop. Refreshments and souvenirs quickly became an essential part of the Festiniog's cash flow. The neighbouring Talyllyn Railway, which had been first into the preservation field, had no rolling stock suitable for this particular job but it did convert an old four-wheel carriage into a mobile tea bar which, shunted into a convenient siding, did duty as a refreshment room at busy times. With the trail thus blazed, the standard gauge preserved

Narrow gauge enterprise: Festiniog Railway buffet car No 103, purpose-built in 1968, in action in 1985. *Author.*

railways made refreshment service an important part of their business, and this was given a tremendous boost by the rescue of some interesting restaurant cars dating back to pre-war days which by luck had survived, in better or worse repair, into British Rail service. In particular, the Severn Valley Railway acquired a pair of former GWR diners that had sunk to the status of engineers' messrooms in South Wales; the Great Central was also well up in the field, renovating one of Gresley's distinctive teak-bodied buffet cars of 1937. There were others including a handful of ex-SR Pullmans on lines in the South, and to make these handsome but costly vehicles earn their keep their owners began to market 'package trips' including not only a steam-hauled return trip on the line, but an excellent dinner with wine as well.

The popularity of these events and the good publicity they gained encouraged British Rail late in 1984 to run the first of what were to become known as the Sunday Luncheon Specials. The formula comprised a train ride in comfortable saloon stock, a historic destination such as Norwich or York, a full roast beef luncheon on the journey and afternoon tea on the way back, for an all-inclusive price. These trains were an immediate and widely-reported hit and the following year, now running from Marylebone, they enjoyed the added bonus of a steam locomotive, this programme covering some summer weekday evenings as well. Here was an area where the old magic of 'dinner in the diner' still held good, and the passengers who flocked to the ticket barrier had little but praise for railway catering, past and present.

Indeed the quality of the food itself on regular main line trains had by and large long ceased to cause complaint, save the occasional hiccups inevitable in any large organisation. What had not fallen off – rather the opposite, in fact – were complaints about the quality and especially the reliability of service. With ever-greater opportunities for travel and eating out, passengers were becoming more and more demanding. At the same time, the fleet of ageing Mk I restaurant cars was as we have seen being hammered into the ground while the new Mk III cars coming in were not proving as reliable as hoped. A particular source of trouble was shortage of spare parts, for the electrical and catering equipment was all specially-designed and built and the manufacturers had no large stock on which to draw.

Against this background the managers of Travellers-Fare had for some years been at work on an entirely new catering system, designed to rid the service of all these shortcomings at one fell swoop. The first evidence of the new approach appeared in 1980 with the mini-buffet trolleys, described in Chapter 5. The basic principle was to prepare the snacks off the train, load them on a trolley, sell them on board from a fixed point and then wheel off the trolley with 'empties' stowed inside, to be replaced by another loaded trolley as necessary.

The possibilities of this system were multiplied almost overnight by the agreement struck in 1984 with the National Union of Railwaymen to operate trolleys unhindered along the full length of corridor trains. Food could now be taken to the customers instead of the other way round, thus giving sales a considerable boost, while that persistent bugbear, the long queue at the buffet counter would be diminished, for trolleys could purvey all buffet snacks except hot items – toasted sandwiches, bacon and egg, and 'Expressburgers.'

The other vital plank of the new plans was the recently-perfected 'cook-chill' system of food preparation. Cook-chill involves preparation off the train of a hot dish – veal jardinière, for example – to a certain state, then chilling it very rapidly using liquid nitrogen to about $+3°C$, at which temperature it will keep perfectly for several days. The dish is then quickly 'regenerated' in a convection or microwave oven immediately before use.

With the preparation taken away from the confines and hazards of the railborne kitchen car all the old limitations on the menu disappeared and there is no technical reason why any meal, however exotic, cannot be prepared and served. Kitchen equipment on the train, too, is much simpler – refrigerators and ranges are eliminated altogether – so with less to go wrong, reliability improves at a stroke. With the political climate of the day demanding more 'private sector' involvement in state industries, outside firms were invited to tender for the jobs of preparing the food for 'Cuisine 2000', as the new system was christened. The first contracts, for the London to Manchester run, went to Trusthouse Forte, supplying from its kitchens at Luton Airport and Ringway (Manchester) respectively – the airlines had already instituted a similar system for their first class passengers.

The railways score over many airlines by using silver service for the main course, matched by new designs of quality china, cutlery and glassware. The place lay-ups are presented to the passenger on trays, and these and all other provisions come aboard on a range of basically similar trolleys which are used for selling, store or displaying food. Dirty plates and dishes go straight into the emptied trolleys, the whole to be collected on a barrow from the train side on arrival. The staff thus have far less afterwork to do, as well as far less preparation, and another old bug-bear, the short time available for serving the customer, is swept away.

The entry of a private firm into train catering, albeit at one remove, was a significant event for main line services. But it had been preceded a couple of years earlier by a handful of local entrepreneurs who, sailing before the political wind, successfully struck local agreements with railway management to begin running mobile trolley services on certain secondary routes. These were the first private services on trains (excluding Pullman) since the demise in 1948 of the old Frederick Hotels

'Cuisine 2000' in its first month of service, on the Euston – Manchester run in August 1985. Place lay-ups having arrived in one trolley, starters for the Great British Breakfast follow on another. *British Rail.*

contracts on the Southern Railway, and the first of them, operating under the name of Gylee Enterprises, began operations between Shrewsbury and Newport in the summer of 1984. Soon there were several in various parts of the country, offering a basic but welcome service on lines where refreshments had hitherto been a luxury unknown. One of these firms, Rightline Caterers of Rhyl in North Wales, was signed up by British Rail's local management to ply on a handful of local services between Chester and Holyhead. But in 1985 Rightline began to cover rather more such trains, and somebody overlooked the fact that during the peak weeks of summer one of these became a through service to London, scheduled for a Travellers-Fare trolley throughout. Sure enough, on the first day of the peak timetable, the two trolleys, private and state enterprise, boarded the train at opposite ends unseen by each other, and somewhere along by Llandudno, in a second class saloon in the middle of the train, they met. The children on board had been hoping a duel might break out, but fortunately good sense prevailed all round and for the next few weeks the two shared the train between them.

Beside the train trolleys, small businesses were also well established on the stations, for as part of the re-shaping of their business Travellers-Fare had for some time been ceding a succession of small station buffets to local private enterprise. Not all of these improved the railway catering image, with old bus seats, cracked teacups and slow service the order of the day; others made up in character what they lacked in finesse, with Manningtree in Essex and Stalybridge in Cheshire two examples of places known for the warm welcome that awaits.

The privatisation of British Transport Hotels in 1982–3 finally freed Travellers-Fare of all the conflicting priorities of the hotel business and the weighty costs of the shared headquarters. The logical step was now for Travellers-Fare to become a Division of British Rail, whose in-house contractor it was, and on 1 January 1982 this took place – though financially the caterers, with their closely-watched balance sheets, remained self-standing. Three years later the new, slimmed-down headquarters moved house once more, when Travellers Fare (now minus its hyphen) abandoned St Pancras Chambers for the offices at Paddington known as Tournament House, leaving its former home empty – though plans are now afoot to turn this magnificent building into an hotel once more.

But with the hotels gone it rapidly became clear that the two operations of Travellers Fare, train and station catering, were themselves just as disparate. One was a highly-specialised restaurateur, inextricably tied to British Rail's Inter-City business; the other, a very profitable fast-food and light-meal operator and publican, with a completely different culture and different markets. In other words, having the two together under a joint headquarters made little more sense than having the catering and hotels together. From 1986 therefore, the logical decision was taken to bring train catering under the direct control of British Rail Inter-City. The great combined organisation that had grown up over a century and a half, from the Garnkirk & Glasgow Railway's Gartsherrie Inn of 1832, through the London & Birmingham's first refreshment rooms of 1838, the building and acquisition of the first hotels, the birth of train catering in 1879, to the nationalisation of the whole in 1948, was now unravelling in a few short years.

But what counts is what the customer gets. Railway stations today offer without doubt a better selection of food and drink than ever before, while train catering, freed at last by modern technology from the many restrictions that have plagued it for a century, stands on the threshold of a new era. For those who work in railway catering times are changing, though they will ever be challenging, and the music-hall jokes, in the nature of music-hall, may be around for a while yet. But the calling of the railway caterer remains an honourable one, with a long history and many more chapters yet to be written. They will surely tell no less of a story than those that have gone before.

Bibliography

The railway history books contain scores of scattered references to catering and hotels, but many are very brief and a few are contradictory. This bibliography lists those consulted in preparing the present volume, plus one or two published since which deal with the geographical or architectural background to the hotels business.

Allen, C. J. *Railways of today.* Warne, 1929.

Barnes, E. G. *The Midland Main Line.* Allen & Unwin, 1969.

Biddle, Gordon *Great Railway Stations of Britain.* David & Charles, 1986.

Biddle, Gordon *Victorian Railway Stations.* David & Charles, 1973.

Biddle, Gordon, with O. S. Nock *Britain's Railway Heritage.* Michael Joseph, 1983.

Bignell, Philippa *Taking the Train*, National Railway Museum/HMSO, 1978.

Bonavia, M. R. *The Four Great Railways.* David & Charles, 1980.

Bonavia, M. R. *The Organisation of British Railways.* Ian Allan, 1971.

Boyd, J. I. C. *Narrow Gauge Rails to Portmadoc.* Oakwood Press, 1949.

Carter, E. F. *Historical Geography of the Railways of Britain.* Cassell, 1959.

Christiansen, Rex, with R. W. Miller *The Cambrian Railways.* David & Charles, 1970.

Currie, J. R. L. *The Northern Counties Railway.* David & Charles, 1973.

Dendy Marshall, C. F. *History of the Southern Railway.* Southern Railway Co., 1936.

Dow, George *Great Central* (3 vols). Locomotive Publishing Co, 1962.

Gloag, John *Victorian Comfort.* David & Charles, 1973.

Grocott, F. W. *The Story of New Street.* BR (LM Region), 1954.

Harrison, D. A. C. *Salute to Snow Hill.* Barbryn Press, 1978.

Jackson, Alan A. *London's Termini.* David & Charles, (2nd edn) 1985.

Jones, Edgar *Penguin Guide to the Railways of Great Britain.* Penguin, 1981.

Kichenside, G. M. *The Restaurant Car.* David & Charles, 1979.

Martin, Don *The Garnkirk & Glasgow Railway.* Strathkelvin District Libraries, 1981.

McDermot, E. T. *History of the Great Western Railway* (new edition). Ian Allan, 1964.

Measom, George *Illustrated Guide to the Great Western Railway.* (1852), Reprinted by Countryside Books, 1983.

Measom, George *Illustrated Guide to the South Eastern Railway.* South Eastern Railway Co, 1858.

Morel, Julian *Pullman.* David & Charles, 1983.

Mulligan, Fergus *150 years of Irish Railways.* Appletree Press, 1983.

O'Mahoney, B. M. E. *Newhaven – Dieppe 1825–1980.* Cappella Publications (Ipswich), 1980.

Radford, J. B. *The American Pullman Cars of the Midland Railway.* Ian Allan, 1984.

Ransome-Wallis, Dr P. *The Snowdon Mountain Railway.* Ian Allan, 1962.

Read, Jan, with Maité Manjon *The Great British Breakfast.* Michael Joseph, 1981.

Rogers, A. E. *A Century of Meals on Railway Wheels.* 1979 (unpublished).

Ruddock, J. G. and R. E. Pearson *The Railway History of Lincoln.* Published by J. G. Ruddock (2nd edn) 1985.

Simmons, Prof Jack *The Railway in Town and Country 1830–1914.* David & Charles, 1986.

Taylor, Derek *Fortune, Fame and Folly – British Hotels and Catering 1878–1978.* Caterer & Hotelkeeper, 1977.

Taylor, Derek with David Bush *The Golden Age of British Hotels.* Northwood Publications, 1974.

Thomas, David St John (general editor) *A Regional History of the Railways of Great Britain.* (14 vols) David & Charles.

Thomas, John *The North British Railway.* David & Charles, 1975.

Thomas, R. H. G. *The Liverpool & Manchester Railway.* Batsford, 1980.

Vallance, H. A. *The Great North of Scotland Railway.* David & Charles, 1965.

Whitehouse, P. B. (general editor) *Railway Relics and Regalia.* Country Life Publications, 1975.

Wrottesley, J. *The Great Northern Railway.* Batsford, 1979.

Articles in various back numbers of the following magazines:
Architectural Review
Caterer & Hotelkeeper
Railway Gazette International
The Railway Magazine
Railway World.

Acknowledgements

Many people have helped in gathering material for this book, but my greatest debt of gratitude is to my many friends and colleagues in railway catering and hotels who, during my time with the business, have helped build up my knowledge of its lore and legend. One in particular stands out: A. E. 'Bert' Rogers of Wembley, retired train catering field manager, whose unpublished history and memoirs *A Century of Meals on Railway Wheels* proved a unique and irreplaceable mine of information. Tragically, Bert died just before work on the present volume received the publisher's green light and I am therefore particularly grateful to his widow, Emily, for allowing me unrestricted access to his papers.

Former railway officers E. K. Portman-Dixon, Ringmer; H. R. Stones, Eastbourne; and Leslie Harrington, Dover; contributed much useful information, as did Don Martin, Kirkintilloch; and John Slater, editor, *The Railway Magazine*. Mark Prior, Hereford; George Gundry, Wimbledon; Arthur Satchwell, Derby; Marjorie Lintott, Winchcombe; and H. W. Jones, Doncaster; assited with research. The following individuals and institutions allowed me the use of their archives, in a number of cases themselves spending some time on obscure historical points:

C. E. N. Childs, Librarian, Brunel University
Gwen Townend, National Railway Museum, York
Tim Bryan, Great Western Railway Museum, Swindon
Peter Bailey, Newhaven Historical Society
The Press Office staff, British Rail, London Midland Region
Public Records Office, Kew
Aberdeen City Library
Bath City Archivist's Office
Brighton Public Library
Cleveland County Library
Eastleigh & District Local History Society
Ewart Library, Dumfries
Highland Regional Library
Humberside County Library
Kent County Library
Leeds City Library
Norfolk County Library
Perth & Kinross District Library
Sidmouth Town Council
Suffolk County Archivist's Office

Thanks are also due to my publisher, David St John Thomas, for his enthusiasm and guidance in getting this project 'on the rails', and finally, but by no means least, to my wife Rosemary for typing and re-typing the manuscript, and for her support during those times when my thoughts were more often out on the line than in kitchens nearer home.

APPENDIX
The Railway Hotels of Britain

This Appendix lists the hotels owned by Britain's railway companies, from their beginning up to the final sale in 1983/4.

Tables A to D summarise, in order of opening as railway establishments, all those hotels which came into the ownership and operation of the 'Big Four' companies at the 1923 Grouping, or subsequently. Opening dates have been checked with local reference sources, in particular the handful which differ from information published elsewhere. The complex pattern of leasing-out, though, remains an incompletely recorded area, especially in the early years.

Table E, and Table F (which is alphabetical), are less definitive; they concern a topic which is really peripheral to this book, and one needing very considerable time and research to document properly. Published material on the subject is presently so sparse, however, that they are included here as an outline of the main establishments involved.

TABLE A
RAILWAY-OWNED LMS TERRITORY HOTELS

Location	Hotel	Railway company	Opened by railway	Origin
London, Euston	Victoria	LBR	Sept1839	New ⎫
London, Euston	Euston	LBR	Dec1839	New ⎭
Furness Abbey	Furness Abbey	Furness	1847	Early 17th Century Manor house
Morecambe	Midland	"Little" North Western	1848	New
Stoke-on-Trent	North Stafford	North Staffs.	1849	New
Birmingham (New Street)	Queens	LNWR	1854	New
Inverness	Station	Highland	1855	New
Derby	Midland	Midland	1862	Built privately 1841
Leeds	Queens	Midland	1863	New
Crewe	Crewe Arms	LNWR	1864	Built privately 1837
Dumfries	Station	GSWR	By 1871	Built privately 18??
Liverpool	North Western	LNWR	1871	New
London, St. Pancras	Midland Grand	Midland	1873	New
Glasgow	St. Enoch	GSWR	1879	New
Holyhead	Station	LNWR	1880	New
Bletchley	Station	LNWR	1881	New
Preston	Park	LNWR+LYR	1882	New
Glasgow	Central	Caledonian	1885	New
Ayr	Station	GSWR	1886	New
Liverpool	Exchange	LYR	1888	New
Perth	Station	Cal+NBR+HR	1889	New
Bradford	Midland	Midland	1890	New
Liverpool	Adelphi	Midland	1892	Built privately 1826 (enlarged 1876)
Kyle of Lochalsh	Lochalsh	Highland	1897	Formerly 'Kyle House' (? an inn)
Edinburgh	Caledonian	Caledonian	1903	New (originally Princes St. Hotel)
Manchester	Midland	Midland	1903	New
Dornoch	Dornoch	Highland	1904	New
Turnberry	Turnberry	GSWR	1906	New
Strathpeffer	Highland	Highland	1911	New
Auchterarder	Gleneagles	Caledonian	1924	New
Stratford on Avon	Welcombe	LMS	1931	Built as private residence 1867
Prestatyn	Prestatyn Holiday Camp	LMS	1939	New
Greenore	Greenore	LNWR/DNGR	1873	New
Dublin	North Western	LNWR	c. 1877	New
Portrush	Northern Counties	Midland/BNCR	1883	Built privately, mid-19th Century
Belfast	Midland Station	Midland/BNCR	1898	New
Larne	Laharna	Midland	1909	Built privately 1883

Disposal	Remarks
ɔsed 1963 and demolished.	Leased out 1839–?1846. Structurally joined 1881.
ɔsed 1938. Partly demolished c. 1950	Open as barracks in World War II.
ld 1952	{ Leased out early as "North Western Hotel". Complete rebuild 1933.
ld 1953	Leased out, 1849–1932. Operated by LMS 1933–53.
ɔsed & demolished 1965/6	Leased out 1856–81. Known as the "N. Western" 1872–81.
ase sold 1983	—
ld 1982	Leased out to Spiers & Pond in early years
ase sold 1984	Contracted out until 1886. Complete rebuild 1937
ld 1952	Lease bought 1864, subsequently freehold also
ld 1972	Leased out when first acquired. Complete rebuild 1897
ɔsed 1933, converted to offices	—
ɔsed 1935, converted to offices	To re-open as an hotel?
ɔsed 1974, demolished 1977	
ɔsed 1951, converted to offices	Station buffet remained open on ground floor until all demolished, 1978
drooms converted to staff accommodation c.1930	Ground floor dining rooms remained open. Demolished c.1965
d 1949, converted to offices	50/50 joint venture LNWR+LYR
ase sold 1983	—
d 1951	—
sed 1971, subsequently demolished	Façade (listed) still extant
d 1983	One-third owned by each of three companies. Extended 1919
sed 1975	Reopened privately 1985. Replaced private Market St. Hotel on site, bought by MR but not operated
d 1983	Complete rebuild 1914
d 1983	Complete rebuild 1932–5
d 1981	—
d 1983	—
d 1965	—
d 1983	—
d 1958	Leased to War Dept. 1940–54 – closed until sale
d 1981	Construction began 1913, interrupted by World War I
d 1983	—
d 1948	Joint Venture with Thos. Cook
sed & sold 1952	—
sed 1922, converted to offices	—
ken over by UTA 1949	Leased in, 1881–1902. Sold by UTA 1966
ken over by UTA 1949	Sold by UTA 1966. Complete rebuild after World War II
ken over by UTA 1949	Sold by UTA 1966

TABLE B
RAILWAY-OWNED
LNER TERRITORY HOTELS

Location	Hotel	Railway company	Opened by railway	Origin
New Holland	Yarborough	Great Grimsby & Sheffield Jct.	1851	New
Hull	Royal Station	NER	1851	New
Peterborough	Great Northern	GNR	1851	New
London, Kings Cross	Great Northern	GNR	1854	New
Newcastle	Royal Station	NER	1854	New
Sheffield	Royal Victoria	MSLR+GNR	1862	New
Saltburn	Zetland	SDR	1863	New
Harwich	Great Eastern	GER	1865	New
Leeds	Great Northern	GNR	1869	New
Hunstanton	Sandringham	GER	1876	New
York	Royal Station	NER	1878	New
Glasgow	North British	NBR	1880	Built c.1780. At one time was "Queens Hotel" (private)
London, Liverpool Street	Great Eastern	GER	1884	New
Parkeston Quay	Great Eastern	GER	1884	New
Grimsby Town	Yarborough	MSLR	1890	Built privately 1851
Grimsby Docks	Royal	MSLR	1890	Built privately 1865 as Royal Dock Hotel
Aberdeen	Palace	GNSR	1891	Built privately 1874
Bradford	Great Northern	GNR	1893	Built privately 1867 as Victoria Hotel
Cruden Bay	Cruden Bay	GNSR	1899	New
Edinburgh	North British	NBR	1902	New
Aberdeen	Station	GNSR	1910	Opened privately 1900
Hartlepool	Grand	NER	1912	Built privately 1901
Felixstowe	Felix	GER	1919	Built privately 1903
London, Marylebone	Great Central	LNER	(1945)	Built privately 1899
St. Andrews	Old Course	BTH	1968	New

Disposal	Remarks
ɔld 1946	Replaced private Yarborough Hotel, purchased by GG&SJR 1845. Currently open as 'Lincoln Castle' pub.
ease sold 1983	Enlarged 1907, rebuilt and further enlarged 1934.
ɔld 1983	
ease sold 1983	Leased out 1854–76
ease sold 1983	Major extensions 1893
ɔld 1982	Joint Venture; MS+LR bought out GNR 1883.
	Leased out 1862–83
ɔld 1976	SDR amalgamated with NER during construction of hotel
ɔld 1923 and converted to Town Hall	Closed 1908–12. Sold again to private owner 1983.
ɔld 1952	{ Replaced private Wellington Hotel on site. { Rebuilt after fire 1906, now Wellesley Hotel
losed 1939, converted to offices etc.	Open as restaurant, bar, and offices, flats etc. from 1950; demolished 1967
ɔld 1983	Replaced first Station Hotel (Table E). Now 'Royal York Hotel'
ease sold 1984	Major rebuild 1895. Now 'Copthorne Hotel'
ease sold 1983	Extended 1901
losed 1963, converted to offices	
ɔld 1951	
ɔld 1949	Demolished 1966
estroyed by fire 1941	Substantially extended c.1894
ɔld 1952	
losed 1939. Demolished 1947–52	
ɔld 1981	
ɔld 1983	
ɔld 1983	Purchased to replace Royal Hotel (qv – Table E)
ɔld 1952 and converted to offices	
onverted to offices 1946	Never served as a hotel after railway purchase. Re-sold 1986. To re-open as hotel?
ɔld 1982	

TABLE C
RAILWAY-OWNED
GWR TERRITORY HOTELS

Location	Hotel	Railway company	Opened by railway	Origin
London, Paddington	Great Western Royal	GWR	1854	New
St. Ives	Tregenna Castle	GWR	1878	Built as private residence 1773
Fishguard	Fishguard Bay	GWR	1898	Built privately as Wyncliff Hotel
Moretonhampstead	Manor House	GWR	1929	Built as private residence 1907
Bath	Grand Pump Room	GWR	1946	Built privately 1869

TABLE D
RAILWAY-OWNED
SR TERRITORY HOTELS

Location	Hotel	Railway company	Opened by railway	Origin
Newhaven	London & Paris	LBSCR	1848	New
Dover	Lord Warden	SER	1853	New
London, Charing Cross	Charing Cross	SER	1865	New
London, Cannon Street	Cannon Street	SER	1867	New (originally City Terminus Hotel)
Eastleigh	Junction	LSWR	1871	Built privately 1841
London, Victoria	Grosvenor	LBSCR	1872	Built privately 1861
Brighton	Terminus	LBSCR	1877	Built privately 1851
London, Holborn	Holborn Viaduct	LCDR	1877	New
Hythe	Imperial	SER	1880	New (originally Seabrook Hotel)
Southampton	South Western	LSWR	1882	Built privately 1872 as the Imperial
Port Victoria	Port Victoria	SER	1883	New
Deal	South Eastern	SER	1901	New
London, Charing Cross	Craven	SER	1911	Built privately as Globe Tavern c.1730
Sidmouth	Knowle	Southern	1947	Built as private residence 1805 Private hotel by 1880's

Disposal	Remarks
...se sold 1983	Leased out 1854–1896 to GW Royal Hotel Co.
...d 1983	Leased out 1878–1895
...way operation ceased 1950	Owned by Fishguard & Rosslare Railways & Harbours Co. 1898–1967. Rebuilt and renamed 1906. Currently open privately
...d 1983	—
...se surrendered 1956. Demolished 1959	Leased-in by GWR while still under Government requisition. Used only for non-residential meetings, exhibitions etc.

Disposal	Remarks
...nverted to barracks/offices 1940	Leased/contracted out throughout. Disused after World War II and demolished 1958
...nverted to offices 1947	Leased out 1896–1940
...ase sold 1983	—
...osed & converted to offices 1931	Leased out 1867–75 and 1890–1912. Destroyed in air raid 1941
...osed c.1966, demolished 1970	Leased out from 1887, through to closure
...ase sold 1983	Leased out from acquisition through to 1977 (lease changed 1899). Rebuilt 1902–08
...osed & demolished (road widening) 1923	Under private lessees 1877–1903; under Bertrams contract thereafter
...nverted to offices after World War I ...quisitioning	Contracted out throughout. Ground floor refreshment rooms open until 1930 when entire building let as offices. Destroyed in air raid 1941
...osed 1939 and subsequently sold	Leased out to Hythe Imperial Hotel Co. – wound up 1941. Now open privately
...osed 1941 and converted to offices	Leased out 1882–1899 and again subsequently. Major rebuild 1925
...osed 1950 and demolished	Contracted out
...ld 1937	Renamed 'Queens Hotel' 1948–77, then closed. Destroyed by fire 1981
...eased out 1954	Terrace building expanded into adjoining houses. Closed c.1963, demolished 1973
...ld 1951	Much enlarged and rebuilt mid-19th century. Converted to offices 1970

TABLE E
SOME HOTELS SOLD OR CLOSED BY RAILWAYS BEFORE 1914

Location	Hotel	Railway Company
Birmingham, Curzon Street	Hardwick's Queens	London & Birmingham
Swindon	Queens Royal	Great Western
Gateshead	Greenesfield Station	Brandling Junction
Folkestone	Pavilion	London & Dover
York	Station	North Eastern
Carlisle	County	Lancaster & Carlisle
West Hartlepool	Royal	North Eastern
Neyland	New Milford	South Wales
London, London Bridge	Terminus	LBSCR
Birmingham, Snow Hill	Great Western	Great Western
Blaenau Festiniog	Queens	LNWR

TABLE F
HOTELS ONCE UNDER PARTIAL OR INDIRECT RAILWAY CONTROL

Location	Hotel	Railway company
Aberystwyth	Queens	Cambrian
Achnasheen	Station	Highland
Alderley Edge	Queens	North Staffs.
Burntisland	Royal	LNER
Colchester	Victoria Station	(Eastern Counties)
Dalkeith	Harrow Inn	LNER
Edinburgh	Crown	LNER
Fleetwood	North Euston	(Preston & Wyre)
Fort Augustus	Lovat Arms	LNER
Glasgow	Ivanhoe	LNER
Heysham	Heysham Tower	Midland
Keighley	Queens	LMS
Keswick	Keswick Hotel	Cockermouth, Keswick & Penrith
Leek	Churnet Valley	North Staffs.
Leek	Rudyard Lake	North Staffs.
Lincoln	Great Northern	GNR
Linlithgow	Star & Garter	LNER
Newquay	Great Western	Great Western
Normanton	Station	Midland
St. Neots	Station	LNER

Built	Remarks
c.1840	Leased out in early years; refreshment rooms on ground floor. Converted to offices by 1900. Demolished 1979
1841	Leased to succession of contractors. Converted to offices by 1900
1844	Integrated with station buildings, originally a private hotel. Converted to offices by 1900
1849	Leased early: sold to Frederick Hotels by 1904. Converted to flats post World War II, replaced by new hotel on site, 1970's
1853	Closed and converted to offices 1878 upon opening of new hotel. Extant as BR(ER) Headquarters
1853	Sold early. Extant as 'Cumbrian Hotel'
1853	Bought by NER by 1880. Closed and converted to offices 1912, upon acquisition of Grand Hotel (qv Table B). Bar remained open.
1861	Sold by GWR 1911.
1861	Built privately, purchased by LBSCR 1893 for conversion to offices. Destroyed in air raid 1941.
1863	Built privately, purchased by GWR 1906 for conversion to offices. Ground floor restaurant remained open. Demolished 1970.
1881	Sold early

Remarks

quired 1913 by Aberystwyth Queens Hotel Co. (formed and controlled by Cambrian Railways)

ilt 1870, integral with station, leased out continuously from opening and remains so today

ned but not operated by LMS (1933 Annual Report)

ned but not operated by LNER between 1923 and World War II

ilt 1843 as separate venture by railway promoter Samuel Peto. Sold 1849 and converted to mental spital.

ned but not operated by LNER between 1923 and World War II

ned but not operated by LNER (1923 Railway Year Book)

ilt 1841 as separate venture by railway promoter Peter Hesketh Fleetwood. Used for a time as itary barracks.

ned but not operated by LNER (1934 Railway Year Book). Currently open privately

ned but not operated by LNER (1934 Railway Year Book)

der Midland Railway control 1896–1919

ned but not operated by LMS in 1920s; closed 1931

ilt 1869 and leased out to Keswick Hotel Co. (formed and controlled by CK & PR). Later sold, currently n privately

ned but not operated by LMS (1933 Annual Report)

d 1924 by LMS

ilt 1848, sold by 1948; demolished 1965. Leased out throughout railway ownership

ned but not operated by LNER between 1923 and World War II

R major shareholder from opening (1878), appointed hotel directors, and offered hotel traffic reduced riage rates

der Midland Railway Management in late 19th/early 20th century. Residential business ceased 1902

ned but not operated by LNER between 1923 and World War II

Index